2005 Christmas

Dear Barnaby,
lots of love
Aunty Ann & Uncle Ian

Ready in minutes

THE COOKBOOK

Photography by Diane & Christoph Heierli   Styling by Abigail Donnelly

The publishers wish to thank the following outlets for their assistance with location, clothing and props for photography:
@ Home, Andiamo's, Boardmans, Clicks, Edgars, LIM, Markhams, Mr Price Home,
The Yellow Door, Village & Life, Woolworths, YDE.

NOTE: Because of the slight risk of salmonella, raw eggs should not be served to the very young,
the ill or elderly, or to pregnant women.

First published in 2005 by Struik Publishers
(a division of New Holland Publishing (South Africa) (Pty) Ltd)
Cape Town • London • Sydney • Auckland
www.struik.co.za

Cornelis Struik House, 80 McKenzie Street,
Cape Town 8001, South Africa
Garfield House, 86–88 Edgware Road,
London W2 2EA, United Kingdom
14 Aquatic Drive, Frenchs Forest, NSW 2086, Australia
218 Lake Road, Northcote, Auckland, New Zealand

New Holland Publishing is a member of
Johnnic Communications Ltd

Reproduction by Hirt & Carter Cape (Pty) Ltd
Printed and bound by Craft (Pte) Ltd, Singapore

10 9 8 7 6 5 4 3 2 1

Publishing Manager: Linda de Villiers
Editor: Joy Clack
Designer: Beverley Dodd
Photographers: Diane and Christoph Heierli
Food Stylist: Abigail Donnelly
Food Stylist's Assistant: Janine du Plessis
Fashion Stylist: Amaria Carstens
Proofreader: Tessa Kennedy

ISBN 1 77007 027 3

www.imagesofafrica.co.za

IMAGES OF AFRICA
PHOTO LIBRARY

Contents

Introduction

There are few activities or interests that have changed and developed so dramatically over the past few decades as that of the food industry. The ever increasing awareness and intrigue over new ingredients, culinary trends and fashions, flavours, textures, temperatures, blends and marriages keep millions entertained and nourished around the world.

With expanding global borders and keen, appreciative palates wishing to sample and experiment with ingredients of other nations, our choice of dishes is probably only limited to imagination, cost and the time it takes to produce them.

We all want to eat healthy, fresh foods and today we are keener than ever to focus on diet, balance, vitamins, GM-free and organic foods, to name but a few. In addition to all this, the demands of a hectic business and social life can result in less time being spent in the kitchen trying to attain these goals, so, with this in mind, I have put together a book that is slightly different to many that we find on offer.

I have moved away from the usual format of starters, fish, meat and dessert, and instead offer a collection of mouthwatering recipes based on the time it takes to cook them. The recipes reflect fresh and fragrant Thai, Vietnamese, Indonesian, Javanese and Burmese influences to stimulate the palate. Indian influences also shine through for the lovers of curry spices, while Spanish, French, British and Italian recipes look after the European contribution. North Africa and Mexico also have a look in.

These are all dishes that I enjoy cooking and eating, depending upon both time and mood. The recipes are all healthy, nutritious and achievable, tried and tested by friends, family and colleagues in both the UK and in South Africa. They are ideal for those individuals who enjoy eating but dislike cooking, as well as the keen food enthusiast ready to impress.

Ready in Minutes also looks after every aspect of the day, from brunch to light lunches and from family meals to dinner parties. And all are geared around the cooking time that we may or may not have. As I have a passion for ingredients, I have included information that I hope may also be of interest to you. I have included the history, nutrition and a few facts that I can't help but come out with in my TV and live shows. So, I hope you find time for *Ready in Minutes* and will be inspired to create your own world of flavours, all in your own good time!

Here's a selection of stunning dishes to try when the weather is too hot or you just don't fancy sweating over a hot stove. Fresh, clean, crisp flavours that could render the oven redundant for weeks!

zero

0

minutes
cooking time

Chilled melon soup
with juniper
Serves 4

A fresh chilled soup for a light meal or a summer appetiser, or even a dessert.

2 ripe ogen (winter) melons, peeled, seeded and roughly chopped

  (you can also use cantaloupes or honeydew melons)

150 ml chilled crisp white wine

30 ml ground fresh juniper berries (available from speciality food stores)

30 ml clear honey

200 ml cold water

150 ml double cream

4 fresh mint leaves

crushed ice (optional) and 4 sprigs fresh mint for serving

1. Place all the ingredients, except the ice and mint sprigs, in a food processor and blitz until smooth.
2. Spoon the crushed ice into chilled serving glasses.
3. Pour the melon soup over the ice and garnish with mint. Serve immediately.

Avocado

What's in a name?

The name derives from the Spanish *aguacate*, via the Aztecs who named it *ahuacatl*, meaning 'testicle tree', a reference to its shape.

Historical notes

- The avocado comes from a tree originating in Central America. The Spanish noted its existence as early as 1519, but it did not become popular until the twentieth century.
- In many producing countries, avocados were given to babies as their first solid food, and were referred to by sailors as midshipman's butter.
- Avocados were planted in the United States around 1833, but commercial production did not take place until the turn of the nineteenth century.

A few facts

- There are over 500 varieties of this tropical tree, which is a member of the laurel family. Some of the fruits are no bigger than a human thumb; others can weigh over a kilogram.
- The shape can differ from that of a pear to that of a sausage.
- The main exporters around the world include Israel, South Africa and Mexico.
- In nature, avocados drop before they ripen. This is due to an inhibiting agent in the leaves that prevents them ripening on the tree.

Health & fitness

- The flesh contains more than 25 per cent fat and has more protein than any other fruit. They may contain up to 400 calories (1 675 kJ) per fruit, so look out if on a diet.
- They are a rich source of: Vitamin E, an anti-oxidant that prevents free radical damage that might lead to cancers; potassium, which controls blood pressure; and Vitamin B, which is necessary for a healthy nervous system and to control morning sickness.

Hints & tips

If an avocado is a little too firm and unripe, place it in a brown paper bag with a ripe banana, then seal the bag. The gases produced by the banana will help to ripen the avocado and it will be ready to eat in less than 24 hours.

Chilled avocado soup
with quick Bloody Mary salsa
Serves 4

Avocado soup

1 large or 2 medium ripe avocados,
    peeled, stoned and roughly chopped
    (you should have 2 full cups)

2 ripe tomatoes, peeled, seeded and
    roughly chopped

75 g spring onions, trimmed and
    roughly chopped

1 large clove garlic, chopped

1 fresh Thai or jalapeno chilli,
    seeded and stem removed

25 g fresh coriander leaves

125 ml fresh lemon juice

50 ml extra virgin olive oil

2.5 ml garam masala

125 ml plain yoghurt

salt and freshly ground black pepper

60 ml crushed ice

Quick Bloody Mary salsa (optional)

3 large vine-ripened tomatoes,
    seeded and chopped

2 fresh Thai or jalapeno chillies,
    seeded and finely chopped

15 ml fresh lime or lemon juice

30 ml fresh coriander leaves

2 cloves garlic, crushed

30 ml extra virgin olive oil

15 ml Worcestershire sauce

5 ml tomato paste

1. To make the soup, place all the ingredients, except the seasoning and ice, into a food processor and blitz until smooth. Season to taste.

2. If you are going to make the salsa, place all the salsa ingredients in a bowl and stir well. (You can make this salsa 8–12 hours ahead and leave it chilled to allow the flavours to intensify.)

3. Add the crushed ice to the soup and stir. If you want to thin out the soup, add a little iced sparkling mineral water or some thin plain yoghurt. Serve in chilled bowls with the Bloody Mary salsa on the side.

Gazpacho

Serves 4–6 (makes about 1.5 litres)

Summer lunch treat! This is one of those dishes that owes everything to the quality of the ingredients. Fresh and simple, a blitz and go. It's also great the following day, as time allows the flavours to fully emerge...so make plenty!

2 slices white bread, crusts removed

3 cloves garlic, roughly chopped

50 ml extra virgin olive oil

500 g medium vine-ripened tomatoes, seeded and
   roughly chopped

1 yellow pepper, seeded and roughly chopped

1 cucumber (about 30 cm), peeled and chopped

1 onion, chopped

30 ml sherry vinegar

250 ml cold water

salt and freshly ground black pepper

1. Place the bread and garlic in a food processor
   and blitz.
2. Add the olive oil and blitz again.
3. Place the tomatoes, yellow pepper, cucumber and
   onion in the food processor and blitz for 1–2 minutes
   until smooth. Pour the mixture into a clean bowl, add
   the vinegar and water and stir well. Season to taste.
4. Cover and place in the refrigerator for 2 hours to chill.
   When ready, pour into chilled bowls or glasses and
   serve, preferably in a sunny and warm environment.

tips

- If the tomatoes have good acidity but lack sweetness, add 5 ml castor sugar when blitzing.
- Add sparkle to the gazpacho by using sparkling water instead of still, and add only seconds before serving.

0 minutes

13

Prawn & mango salad
with spiced ginger dressing
Serves 4

A fresh and healthy lunchtime salad.

2 mangoes, peeled and stoned
   (if unavailable, use papaw)
½ cucumber, peeled and thinly sliced
400 g large prawns, cooked
   and peeled
12 fresh mint leaves

Spiced ginger dressing
5 cm piece fresh root ginger, grated
juice of 1 lemon
½ fresh chilli, seeded and
   finely chopped
15 ml soy sauce
30 ml peanut oil
30 ml hazelnut or sesame oil
2.5 ml freshly ground black pepper

1. To make the salad, slice the mangoes into thin, manageable slithers and place in a serving bowl with the slices of cucumber.
2. Add the prawns and gently mix together.
3. To prepare the dressing, whisk all the ingredients together until well combined.
4. Drizzle the dressing over the salad and lightly mix together. Sprinkle with mint and serve.

Sweet-&-Sour salad

Serves 4

This is one of my favourite salads, with a blend of ingredients that stimulates all the senses. The balance between sweet, fresh and clean flavours mixed with aromas of fragrant mint are all brought to life with the zesty kick of fresh lime and a stimulating punch of chilli. Texture is also important – a combination of smooth soft slices of mango and a satisfying crunch of peanuts.

½ cucumber, peeled and thinly sliced

2 pears, peeled, cored and thinly sliced

4 spring onions, finely sliced

30 ml chopped fresh mint

30 ml chopped peanuts

1 mango, peeled, stoned and thinly sliced

extra mint for serving

Dressing

1 clove garlic, crushed

10 ml muscovado (dark brown) sugar

30 ml Thai fish sauce (nam pla)

juice of 1 lime

1 fresh chilli, seeded and finely chopped

15 ml rice wine vinegar (available from speciality or Asian food stores)

15 ml sesame oil

1. Make the dressing first. Mix all the dressing ingredients together and set aside.
2. To make the salad, place all the salad ingredients in a bowl and coat with the dressing.
3. Mix thoroughly, then transfer the salad to a serving bowl.
4. Scatter with a few mint leaves and serve.

0 minutes

Thai papaya salad

Serves 4–6

Fresh, healthy and very, very tasty. The skill in making this is ensuring that you have fresh and tasty ingredients. The rest is putting it into a bowl and serving!

1 lettuce or mixed salad leaves for
   four to six portions – mustard
   greens, watercress, herbs and
   flowers are good for colour,
   texture and flavour
2 papayas (papaws), peeled, seeded
   and thinly sliced
2 vine-ripened tomatoes, thinly sliced
175 g peeled and cooked shrimps
   or prawns
1 clove garlic, finely chopped
2 fresh green chillies, seeded and
   finely chopped
60 ml fresh lime or lemon juice
30 ml Thai fish sauce (nam pla)
30 ml white wine vinegar
15 ml castor sugar
15 ml light soy sauce
30 ml roasted peanuts, lightly
   crushed

1. Place a bed of lettuce in individual serving bowls
   (or one large salad bowl).
2. Combine the papayas, tomatoes, shrimps or prawns,
   garlic and chilli in a mixing bowl.
3. In a separate bowl, mix together the lime or lemon
   juice, fish sauce, vinegar, castor sugar and soy sauce,
   and stir until the sugar has dissolved.
4. Pour the dressing over the salad leaves and toss the
   salad to coat it in the dressing.
5. Spoon the papaya, prawn and tomato mix on top
   of the leaves and sprinkle with the roasted peanuts.
   Serve immediately.

hint

When preparing a salad, avoid mixing it with dressing
until just before serving, otherwise the acidic content
in the dressing will start to 'cook' the delicate leaves,
making them soggy and unappetising.

Pear & watercress salad
with blue cheese dressing

Serves 4–6

This salad (or side dish) is a mix of the fruity flavour of the pear and the spicy flavours of the pepper and the watercress, seasoned with a creamy cheese dressing.

2 bunches (about 90 g) fresh watercress, trimmed and washed

3 pears, cored and thinly sliced

150 g toasted hazelnuts, coarsely chopped

juice of 1 lemon

75 ml hazelnut oil (available from speciality food stores)

15 ml red wine vinegar

freshly ground black pepper

250 g Gorgonzola cheese, plus extra chunks to garnish

1. Place the washed watercress into a bowl and add the pears, hazelnuts and lemon juice. Toss the salad and divide among four to six serving bowls.
2. Place the hazelnut oil, vinegar, pepper and Gorgonzola into a food processor and blitz until smooth and well blended.
3. Pour the dressing over the salads and garnish with chunks of Gorgonzola. Serve immediately.

NB: No salt is needed, as the cheese will be salty enough.

0 minutes

18

Mango

What's in a name?

The name possibly comes from the Tamil for fruit tree, via the Portuguese *manga* or from the Malay *mang*, meaning tree.

Historical notes

- India is the native land of the mango, where it has flourished for several thousand years. It also features largely in Indian mythology and in Buddhist rituals.
- The Portuguese took mangoes to the West Indies, Africa and Brazil in the sixteenth century and they are still cultivated in these countries. Today, South Africa is a major producer and world supplier.

A few facts

- Mangoes belong to the same family as cashew and pistachio nuts.
- The fruits vary in size, from tiny egg-shaped wild varieties to the large sweet ones.
- There are over 2 500 different varieties.
- In India, they are usually picked before they are ripe to make tarts and preserves.

Health & fitness

- Mangoes are extremely rich in vitamins A, B and C. They are, however, quite high in sugar and a medium-sized fruit contains around 14 per cent sugar.
- It is advisable to drink neither milk, water nor alcohol for up to two hours after eating a mango, as this may cause stomach pains. These pains are not dangerous, but may be uncomfortable for the unfortunate few.

Hints & tips

- Store ripe mangoes in the refrigerator; this will keep them fresh for 4–6 days.
- If the mangoes are firm, keep them at room temperature until softened.
- Take care not to get mango juice onto clothing, as it can stain.

Mango & crab spring rolls
with chilli dipping sauce

Serves 4 (2 rolls per person)

These spring rolls are good to eat and also healthy as they are very low in fat. They don't need cooking as the rice paper merely needs soaking in cold water to soften. The only challenge that you may have is with the rolling process. This can take several attempts so don't be disappointed if they do not turn out perfectly on your first go. Remember not to be tempted to over-fill each roll.

Spring rolls

8 rice paper circles (20 cm diameter)

25 g fresh mint leaves

1 carrot, peeled and grated

2 mangoes, peeled, stoned, and
  thinly sliced

100 g sun-dried tomatoes in olive oil,
  drained and cut into thin strips

125 g fresh bean sprouts

15 g fresh basil leaves (purple variety
  if available)

100 g cooked white flaky crab meat

4 spring onions, finely shredded

Chilli dipping sauce

30 ml light soy sauce

15 ml castor sugar

15 ml sushi vinegar

5 ml grated ginger

1 clove garlic, crushed

1 fresh red Thai chilli, seeded and
  finely sliced

10 ml sweet chilli sauce

15 ml Thai fish sauce (nam pla)

1. To make the spring rolls, lay a clean tea towel on the work surface. Lay a sheet of rice paper on the tea towel and brush the rice paper thoroughly with water. (Alternatively, dip the rice paper into cold water, then lay flat on the tea towel.) Leave for 1–2 minutes to soften.

2. When the rice paper is soft and pliable, place mint leaves over the bottom two-thirds of the paper, leaving a 2.5 cm border of the rice paper at the base.

3. Place 15 ml grated carrot over the mint leaves, followed by 2 slices of mango, strips of sun-dried tomatoes, some bean sprouts, basil leaves, 15 ml crab meat, spring onions and another layer of fresh mint.

4. Fold up the bottom 2.5 cm border of rice paper and fold it over the filling.

5. Fold in the right- and left-hand side edges of the paper. Continue folding until a tight cylinder is formed.

6. To make the chilli dipping sauce, mix together all the ingredients in a bowl.

7. Just before serving, cut the spring rolls in half – at an angle for added effect – and serve with the dipping sauce on the side.

Fresh line fish
'cooked' in a citrus marinade
Serves 4

Good for an evening dinner party or light luncheon.

NB: You will need to allow about 4 hours' marinating time.

900 g fresh line fish (Cape salmon, halibut and butterfish work
   particularly well)
2 medium onions, thinly sliced
125 ml extra virgin olive oil
250 ml fresh lemon juice
450 g fresh tomatoes, skinned, seeded and quartered
2 bay leaves
30 ml pitted and sliced black olives
5 ml chilli powder
250 ml dry white wine
flat-leaf parsley, rocket and watercress for serving

1. Slice the fish as thinly as possible, so that you can almost see
   through it.
2. Mix together the remaining ingredients, except the parsley, rocket and
   watercress, in a wide, non-metallic bowl.
3. Place the fish in the marinade and leave for around 4 hours in the
   refrigerator. The acids from the lemon juice will start to cook into the
   flesh and the ingredients will start to penetrate and flavour the fish.
   I recommend that you only use the freshest fish for this delicious,
   healthy dish.
4. When ready to serve, place a selection of parsley, rocket and
   watercress in a serving bowl. Place the slices of fish over the
   leaves, then coat with a little of the marinade.
5. Serve with crusty bread and a little Quick Spring Onion Relish
   (page 112).

Berries in Van der Hum
with mascarpone

Serves 4

This is an extremely simple dish to prepare and serve, and is one of those desserts that can be knocked up in minutes yet looks like you have spent hours in the kitchen. Served in stunning glasses, it is bound to impress family and friends.

500 g mixed fresh berries
(e.g. strawberries, Cape
gooseberries, blackberries,
blueberries), washed and hulled
(You can also use a bag of mixed
frozen berries if fresh are out of
season.)
100 g castor sugar
350 ml Van der Hum or any
orange-flavoured liqueur
2 egg whites
300 g mascarpone cheese
icing sugar for dusting

1. Place the berries, castor sugar and Van der Hum into a bowl and leave to marinate for 10–15 minutes.
2. While the berries are marinating, whisk the egg whites in a clean bowl until light and firm peaks are formed.
3. Beat the mascarpone, then fold in the whisked egg whites.
4. Chill four glasses and spoon in some of the berry and Van der Hum mixture. Top with a layer of mascarpone.
5. Finish off with a dusting of icing sugar.

tip

If preferred, serve in tall glasses and repeat the layers of berries and mascarpone three or four times until an attractive, alternating layer effect has been formed.

0 minutes

Coffee

What's in a name?

There are many possible origins to the word coffee. The coffee bush originated in Ethiopia, so the name could be derived from 'Kaffa', a province of this country. Arabs were some of the first people to grow and trade in coffee, so the name could come from the Arabic *qahwa*, meaning wine, as the coffee beans may have been compared to grapes. The Dutch were the first Europeans to cultivate the beans, so it could even originate from their word for it: *kiffie*.

Historical notes

An Ethiopian legend has it that coffee was discovered in the seventh or eighth century by a goatherd, who noticed that his goats became very lively after nibbling the berries. He informed the local monastery of this behaviour, and the monks in turn tried the berries for themselves. They found that it kept them awake, which proved very beneficial during their nightlong prayers. By the eleventh century, the coffee beans had found their way into the hands of Arab traders.

A few facts

- It takes up to 4 500 berries from the Arabica coffee plant to produce just 1 kg of coffee. And since each berry contains two beans, you're looking at 9 000 beans per kilogram!
- An average cup of coffee contains around 75–100 mg of caffeine, compared with around 50 mg in tea and 40 mg in a cola drink.

Health & fitness

Coffee stimulates alertness and contains a tiny amount of niacin (a B vitamin that lowers cholesterol), but those are about its only benefits. Unfortunately, coffee has been linked to increased risk of heart disease, it can cause migraines, and it contains at least 300 other active ingredients that can prove harmful if the coffee is left to stand or brew for even a short time.

Hints & tips

- For the best coffee, grind the beans at the very last moment, as oxidation takes place as soon as the molecules are exposed to air, which reduces the aroma and taste.
- If you do need to store ground coffee, then try storing it in the refrigerator in the tightly sealed block in which it was purchased or, if loose, seal it tightly in a bag and place in the freezer.

Coffee tiramisu

Serves 4–6

A perfect pick-me-up!

3 medium eggs, separated

30 ml castor sugar

500 g mascarpone cheese

350 ml strong black coffee, cooled

75 ml sweet Marsala or Kahlúa coffee liqueur

45 ml brandy

200 g packet ready-made sponge fingers or *langue de chat* biscuits (you need about 18)

50 g dark chocolate, finely grated

5 ml cocoa powder for dusting

1. Whisk together the egg yolks and castor sugar until pale and creamy.
2. Whisk in the mascarpone until combined.
3. In a clean, separate bowl, whisk the egg whites to form stiff peaks.
4. Gently fold the egg whites into the mascarpone mixture and set aside.
5. Divide the sponge fingers or biscuits among 4 x 250 ml or 6 x 200 ml serving glasses, breaking to fit neatly and pressing down if necessary.
6. Mix together the coffee, liqueur and brandy and pour the mixture over the biscuits in each glass.
7. Spoon over a layer of the mascarpone mixture and flatten gently with the back of the spoon.
8. Repeat the process two or three times with the remaining biscuits and mascarpone mixture, finishing with a layer of mascarpone.
9. Cover and place in the refrigerator for at least 1 hour.
10. When ready to serve, sprinkle grated chocolate over the mascarpone and dust with the cocoa powder.

NB: These little desserts can be made up to 24 hours in advance, which will improve their flavour. However, if you're like most people, you will probably tuck into them straight away.

Eaton Mess

Serves 4

Use fresh, frozen or tinned strawberries for this easy dessert.

450 g strawberries

575 ml whipping cream

6 medium, ready-made meringues,
   broken into small pieces

sprigs of mint to decorate and icing
   sugar for dusting

1. Mash the strawberries with a fork or slice thickly.
2. Whip the cream until it forms stiff peaks and fold in the strawberries and most of the broken meringue.
3. Scoop into chilled serving bowls, top with a little broken meringue and a sprig of mint.
4. Chill in the refrigerator for 5 minutes. When ready, dust over the icing sugar and serve.

Peach & amaretti trifle

Serves 4

5 ripe peaches, peeled (optional),
   halved and stoned

120 ml sweet Marsala

175 g amaretti biscuits

300 ml fresh or ready-made custard

250 g mascarpone cheese

150 ml double cream

1. Thinly slice four of the peaches, then soak the slices in the Marsala for 1 hour (this is the preferred soaking time, but it can be less if you're in a hurry).
2. Drain the liquid from the peaches (reserve the Marsala), then spoon half the slices into the base of four serving glasses or one large glass bowl.
3. Dip half the amaretti biscuits into the leftover Marsala and arrange in a layer on top of the peaches.
4. Whisk together the custard and mascarpone, then pour half this mixture over the biscuits.
5. Arrange the remaining peach slices over the custard.
6. Dip the remaining amaretti biscuits into the liquor and arrange over the peaches.
7. Spoon the remaining custard mixture over the biscuits.
8. Gently whip the cream until slightly thickened and dollop or pipe it over the custard.
9. Slice the remaining peach and use it for decoration.

0 minutes

Indian mango fool

Serves 4

2 ripe mangoes, peeled, halved
   and stoned

juice and zest of 1 lime

15 ml castor sugar

50 ml double cream

250 ml plain yoghurt

5 ml rose-water (optional)

hazelnuts or green pistachios
   to decorate

1. Chop up the mangoes into bite-sized pieces and place in a bowl. Add the lime juice, lime zest and castor sugar to the mango.
2. In a separate bowl, whisk the cream to soft peak stage and add the yoghurt.
3. If using, add the rose-water and whisk again.
4. Fold in the mango.
5. Spoon the mixture into four serving glasses, and decorate with the nuts. Serve immediately.

Lemon grass syllabub

Serves 4

The ginger in this recipe works well with the lemon grass to give a gentle bite and warmth at the back of the throat.

280 ml double cream or
   crème fraîche

15 ml icing sugar

30 ml lemon grass cordial*

45 ml dry white wine

grated zest and juice of ½ lemon

4 pieces preserved root ginger,
   thinly sliced, and extra lemon
   zest to decorate

1. Place the cream or crème fraîche in a mixing bowl and whisk in the icing sugar until combined.
2. In a jug, mix together the cordial, wine, lemon zest and juice.
3. Gently and gradually pour the wine mixture into the cream, whisking until the cream just holds its shape.
4. Spoon the dessert into wine glasses and top with the preserved ginger and the zest. Serve immediately.

* To make the cordial, place 300 ml water, 200 g castor sugar, 3 x 12 cm lengths lemon grass, grated 2 cm piece fresh root ginger, and the juice and zest of 1 lemon in a pan and heat gently, stirring, until the sugar dissolves. Increase the heat and simmer for 3–4 minutes until thickened. Cool, then strain.

Lettuce

What's in a name?

Lettuce comes from the Latin – via old French – *lac*, meaning milk. This is a reference to the liquid that oozes out from the stem area when cut.

Historical notes

Lettuce, which is native to the Middle East, was a favourite food of the Greeks, Persians and Romans – although the lettuce of that time would have been tall and spindly. By 500 BC, it was one of the most popular vegetables in Italy. The Chinese have been cultivating it since the fifth century and it was Christopher Columbus who introduced it to America.

A few facts

Lettuce (*Lactuca sativa*) is a plant from the daisy family and is a relative of chicory and dandelion. There are many varieties, but most fall into four main groups:

- Round or butterhead – light green in colour with soft, loose leaves, such as Tom Thumb.
- Crisp head – cabbage-like with tightly packed leaves, such as Iceberg.
- Long leaf – darker green, oblong in shape with crisp leaves, such as Cos or Romaine.
- Loose leaf – vary in colour, rounded in shape with no head, and may include Oak Leaf, Frizzy and Lollo Rosso.

Health & fitness

- Lettuce always seems to be associated with dieting! This is due to the fact it is low in calories, providing it is not coated with an oily or creamy dressing.
- Lettuce is a good source of folate (folic acid) and betacarotene; folate is beneficial during pregnancy and betacarotene for the prevention of degenerative diseases such as cancers.
- It is interesting to note that lettuce varieties with dark green leaves may contain anything up to 50 times more betacarotene than varieties with paler leaves.

Hints & tips

- To crisp up limp lettuce, place it in a pan of cold water in the refrigerator for 45 minutes, then drain and return it to the refrigerator for 20 minutes.
- Lettuce keeps longer if stored on paper in a chilled compartment.

Fresh crisp salad

Serves 4

Fresh and clean. By itself or as an accompaniment.

450 g mixed salad leaves – use a
selection of four varieties from
the following: baby bok choy,
baby spinach, escarole (Batavian
endive), oak leaf, lambs, mustard
greens, watercress

50 g fresh flat-leaf parsley, washed
and dried

50 g picked fresh chervil leaves

50 g fresh chives, snipped

flowers (optional): chive flowers,
pansies, rosemary flowers,
thyme flowers

1. Separate the salad leaves and wash thoroughly in a
bowl of cold water. Dry carefully.
2. Place the salad leaves and herbs into a serving bowl.
3. If entertaining, add some flowers – these will add
flavour and turn the salad into a feast for the eyes.
4. Serve on its own or with one of the dressings given
below or on page 34.

Green goddess dressing

*This dressing was apparently created in honour of actor George Arliss, who
stayed at a particular hotel in San Francisco while starring in a play called
The Green Goddess.*

4 anchovy fillets

30 ml chopped fresh flat-leaf parsley

15 ml chopped fresh tarragon

100 ml mayonnaise

30 ml white wine vinegar

30 ml snipped fresh chives

2.5 ml freshly ground black pepper

Blitz all the ingredients together and drizzle over the salad.
This dressing will keep in the refrigerator for up to a week.

Alan's summer dressing
– quick & oil free

30 ml clear honey

125 ml fresh orange juice

15 ml fresh lime juice

grated zest of ½ orange

5 ml snipped fresh chives

5 ml finely chopped fresh tarragon

salt and freshly ground black pepper

5 ml finely chopped fresh flat-
   leaf parsley

Mix together the honey, orange juice and lime juice, then add all the remaining ingredients and whisk until combined. This dressing is great if on a diet as it does not compromise flavour. It will keep in the refrigerator for up to a week.

Lemon & coriander dressing

125 ml fresh lemon juice

30 ml honey

15 ml roughly chopped fresh coriander

5 ml roughly chopped fresh flat-
   leaf parsley

5 ml roughly chopped fresh tarragon

15 ml extra virgin olive oil

Mix together all the ingredients. Only dress the salad at the last minute, otherwise the acid within the lemon will start to cook the leaves. This dressing is a good accompaniment to fish dishes and will keep in the refrigerator for up to a week.

Honey-mustard dressing

5 ml whole grain mustard

5 ml clear honey

150 ml sunflower oil

juice of ½ lemon

juice, zest and chopped segments
   of ½ orange

Place all the ingredients in a jar and shake vigorously. This dressing is good with grilled, barbecued or fried meat dishes. It will keep in the refrigerator for up to a week.

Fresh, fast food at its best. Why spend hours cooking when healthy and tasty dishes like these can be cooked in minutes?

five
5.
minutes
cooking time

Chargrilled tropical fruit
with chilli crab salad

Serves 4–6

Light lunch...fresh and fruity.

25 ml butter

5 ml castor sugar

1 small pineapple, peeled, trimmed
 and cored

1 large mango, peeled and stoned

1 fresh red chilli, seeded and
 finely chopped

3 spring onions, finely sliced

a few fresh coriander leaves

juice of 1 lime

fresh herbs of choice or paprika
 to garnish

Chilli crab salad

30 ml crème fraîche

1 fresh red chilli, seeded and
 finely sliced

15 ml chopped fresh flat-leaf parsley

juice and zest of 1 lemon or ½ lime

1 stick crisp celery, finely chopped

220 g cooked white crab meat

1. To prepare the chargrilled fruit, melt the butter and dissolve the sugar in the butter in a microwave or over heat in a small pan.
2. Cut the pineapple and mango into equal-sized slices or pieces.
3. Brush the fruit with the sweetened butter mixture.
4. Heat a griddle pan until very hot, then add the fruit carefully, laying it over the griddle lines to obtain a striped effect.
5. Chargrill the fruit on both sides for 30–90 seconds per side.
6. Remove from the heat and place in a bowl with the chilli, spring onions, coriander and lime juice. Toss gently.
7. To make the chilli crab salad, mix together all the ingredients.
8. To serve, divide the fruit among four to six plates and arrange neatly.
9. Divide the crab salad into equal-sized portions and place it on top of the fruit.
10. Garnish with fresh herbs or a light dusting of paprika.

5 minutes

Warm banana
& red onion salad
Serves 4

This salad goes well with curries and spiced dishes.

3 unripe bananas

3 medium red onions, sliced into rings (you can use white onions if red are
unavailable, but these will be a little stronger and not quite as sweet)

1 clove garlic, crushed

juice of 2 limes

2 small fresh chillies, seeded and finely chopped

5 ml clear honey

salt and freshly ground black pepper

50 ml extra virgin olive oil

50 g fresh mint, shredded

1. Peel the bananas and poach them in a little boiling water for
   about 4 minutes until soft.
2. Place the onion slices in a bowl.
3. Add the garlic, lime juice, chillies and honey and stir well.
   Season with salt and pepper.
4. When the bananas have softened, remove carefully and slice at
   an angle.
5. Add the warm banana to the onion mixture and pour over the olive
   oil. Sprinkle over the fresh mint and mix the salad together gently
   and carefully.
6. Transfer to a warmed serving bowl and serve immediately.

Tempura of king prawns
with mint & chilli chutney

Serves 4

This quick and easy dish makes a great appetiser or party nibble.

about 1.5 litres oil for deep-frying

40 g cornflour

40 g plain (cake) flour

5 ml baking powder

25 ml sunflower oil

about 175 ml cold sparkling water

2.5 ml each salt and freshly ground
   black pepper

12–16 king prawns, deveined

extra 45 ml plain (cake) flour
   for dusting

Mint & chilli chutney

1 ml coriander seeds, crushed

25 g fresh mint leaves

4 spring onions

1 fresh green chilli, seeded and
   chopped

15 ml tamarind liquid or juice
   of ½ lime

10 ml castor sugar

1 ml garam masala

60 ml water

1. Heat the oil in a deep-fryer, large pan or a wok to 180–190 °C.*
2. To make the batter, mix together the cornflour, the 40 g plain flour and baking powder in a medium-sized bowl.
3. Add the 25 ml oil and just enough sparkling water to make a smooth, runny batter. Season with salt and pepper.
4. Dust the raw prawns with the extra flour and then dip them into the batter.
5. Fry until crisp, turning occasionally. The cooking time should be around 2 minutes.
6. When the prawns are ready, remove them with a slotted spoon and place onto kitchen paper to drain off any excess oil.
7. To make the chutney, place all the chutney ingredients in a food processor and blitz.
8. Serve the prawns with the chutney alongside in a dipping bowl.

* If you don't have a deep-fryer or fat thermometer, add a cube of bread to the hot oil to test whether it is ready. It should brown within 30 seconds.

tip

The mint and chilli chutney also goes well as a dip for crudités.

Tuna

What's in a name?
The word tuna comes from *atun*, the Spanish word for this fish.

Historical notes
Tuna was a favourite food of the Phoenicians, who used to smoke it, as well as preserve it with salt. In ancient Greece and Rome, it was cooked over open coals and drizzled with oil.

A few facts
- Tuna are grouped among the heavyweights of the sea. They are warm blooded, so need to be constantly on the move to supply sufficient oxygen for themselves. It is this continuous exercise that develops the darkness of the muscle tissue.
- There are five main species of this oily fish, which belongs to the mackerel family:
  - Albacore, a small fish weighing about 35 kg and a firm favourite with the canning industry.
  - Bigeye. This fish can reach 100 kg+ and has a pale flesh that is of excellent eating quality.
  - Yellow fin, probably the most well-known variety, is the species most readily available in the marketplace, both fresh and frozen.
  - Blue fin, the biggest of them all, averaging 300–400 kg, is found in the Atlantic and Pacific oceans. The Japanese are fond of this variety for its use in sashimi.
  - Skipjack, a fish of about 2 kg, got its name from its habit of skipping along the ocean's surface when chasing prey. This one is also a popular choice for the canning industry.

Health & fitness
- Fresh tuna is rich in Vitamin D (good for skin, teeth and bones), Vitamin B12 (good for blood cells) and Omega 3 fatty acids (maintains cell membranes).
- Tinned tuna retains its high vitamin content, but is a poor source of Omega 3 as most of the fish oil is removed before canning. A 100 g portion in vegetable oil contains more than twice the calories as tuna in brine, but the levels of sodium are almost identical.

Hints & tips
Care should be taken when cooking tuna as it can easily toughen and dry out if cooked for too long. Tuna is best served pink or underdone.

Flash-seared tuna cakes
with warm Oriental salad

Serves 4

A fantastic lunch or summer dinner. Fresh, fresh fish is so important as this dish is simply flashed and is as close as you can get to warm sushi.

Tuna cakes

450 g tuna, skinned and deboned

2.5 ml cayenne pepper

30 ml soy sauce

30 ml extra virgin olive oil

zest and juice of 1 lemon

30 ml chopped capers

60 ml peanut or corn oil

100 g sesame seeds

Warm Oriental salad

½ cucumber (about 15 cm),
  peeled and sliced into thin strips

2 spring onions, shredded

50 g fresh coriander leaves

15 fresh mint leaves, shredded

2 fresh red chillies, seeded and
  chopped

50 g fresh flat-leaf parsley, chopped

juice of 2 limes

50 g fresh chives, snipped

60 ml Thai fish sauce (nam pla)

15 ml palm or light brown sugar

30 ml sesame oil

100 g baby spinach leaves

1. Finely chop or coarsely blitz the tuna in a food processor and place in a clean bowl.
2. Add the cayenne pepper, soy sauce, olive oil, lemon juice, zest and the capers to the tuna and mix well.
3. Divide the mixture into four equal-sized portions and form into balls.
4. Flatten the balls to form little cakes.
5. Heat the peanut or corn oil in a heavy-based pan.
6. Roll the tuna cakes in the sesame seeds until well coated.
7. Place the cakes in the hot pan and cook until golden brown on both sides.*
8. While the tuna cakes are frying, prepare the salad by mixing together all the ingredients.
9. Heat a wok and quickly add the salad.
10. Stir-fry for about 45 seconds, then remove from the heat and serve immediately with the tuna cakes.

* For a cool, raw centre, cook for only 90 seconds on each side.

Goat's cheese bruschetta
with black cherry jam

Serves 4

Goat's cheeses have always been a favourite of mine. I enjoy their rustic flavour and they often tend to be hand-produced, holding a charm and personality that has been influenced by the cheesemaker. The soft cheese on crispy bread topped with sweet cherry jam is simply a marriage made in heaven.

4 slices country bread (e.g. plain rustic, Italian bread or ciabatta)

3 large cloves garlic, peeled

60 ml extra virgin olive oil

60 ml red pesto

300 g soft goat's cheese

200 g jar roasted peppers, chopped

20 fresh basil leaves

freshly ground black pepper

black cherry jam for serving

1. Place the sliced bread under a preheated grill and toast on both sides.
2. When cool enough to handle, rub the slices all over with the cloves of garlic.
3. Drizzle with a little olive oil, then spread with red pesto.
4. In a clean bowl, use a fork to mash together the goat's cheese, a little more olive oil, the roasted peppers, basil and black pepper, until relatively smooth.
5. Spoon the mixture onto the toasted bread and place back under the grill for 2–3 minutes.
6. Serve topped with the black cherry jam.

5 minutes

Baked figs
with Parma ham & blue cheese
Serves 4

A fab appetiser – easy and very tasty.

12 fresh figs

175 g Parma ham

225 g blue cheese of choice, cut into small cubes

30 ml olive oil

freshly ground black pepper

chives to garnish

Caper dressing

150 ml sour cream

juice of ½ small lemon

5 ml Dijon mustard

30 ml capers, drained and roughly chopped

1. Preheat the oven to 200 °C.
2. Carefully trim the stalk and slice a thin sliver off the base of each fig.
3. Make a small incision at the top end of the fig, cutting halfway down.
4. Give the fig a quarter turn, then make a second incision through the fig. Repeat for all the figs.
5. Open the figs gently and place on a baking tray.
6. Carefully remove the thin layer of fat from the Parma ham and keep aside.
7. Cut the remaining Parma ham into very thin slices and gently stuff it into the centre of the figs.
8. Place a piece of cheese on the top of the ham and close up the fig as much as possible.
9. Wrap the reserved ham fat around the figs, taking care to ensure an attractive finish.
10. Drizzle the figs with a little olive oil, season with black pepper and place in the oven for about 5 minutes, or until the ham has crisped slightly and the figs have softened, but are still holding their shape.
11. To make the caper dressing, mix together all the dressing ingredients.
12. As soon as the figs are done, serve immediately topped with the caper dressing and garnish with chives.

5 minutes

46

Yoghurt

What's in a name?

The word is derived from the Turkish *yoghurt*, possibly because it was introduced to the rest of Europe from this part of the world.

Historical notes

- Yoghurt is one of the oldest known foods. It was used by the ancient Egyptians and Israelites, and was taken east to India by Arab traders.
- It is thought that yoghurt was first introduced to Europe around the sixteenth century, but it was mostly confined to monasteries and the country of Bulgaria, where it was proclaimed as the elixir of life due to the longevity of tough, yoghurt-eating Bulgarians.
- In 1515, King Francis I of France was prescribed fermented sheep's milk by his doctor, who thought that it would cure him of his depression.

A few facts

- Yoghurt is a cultured product, produced by fermenting milk with bacteria. The most common bacteria used are *Lactobacillus bulgaricus* and *Streptococcus thermophilus*.
- To make yoghurt, milk is heated to destroy any unwanted micro-organisms, then the yoghurt is started by adding the chosen bacteria. It is kept warm at around 44 °C until set.
- Bio-yoghurt is milder and creamier than ordinary yoghurt, due to different live cultures being used, namely *Bifidus* and *Acidophilus*.

Health & fitness

- Yoghurt is a useful source of calcium and phosphorus, and vitamins B2 and B12, all of which are good for strong teeth and a healthy nervous system.
- Yoghurt with live cultures has many benefits, including the control of harmful bacteria in the gut and reducing bad breath associated with digestive disorders.
- Eating yoghurt with live cultures after taking a course of antibiotics will help restore the body's beneficial bacteria that may have been destroyed by the medication.

Hints & tips

If you have used too much chilli or too many hot spices in a dish, add yoghurt to cool things down.

47

Punjabi-style dumplings
in yoghurt sauce

Serves 4

A tasty vegetarian dish.

1.5 litres corn or vegetable oil

2.5 ml bicarbonate of soda

10 ml ground cumin

300 g chickpea flour

5 ml salt

180 ml water

Yoghurt sauce

60 g butter or ghee

1 medium onion, sliced

5 ml grated fresh root ginger

2.5 ml ground cumin

2.5 ml ground cinnamon

1 ml ground cloves

2.5 ml ground cardamom

50 g chickpea flour

150 ml water

250 ml plain, full-cream yoghurt

30 ml chopped fresh basil

15 ml chopped fresh mint

1 fresh chilli, seeded and finely chopped

1. Preheat the oil in a deep-fryer or large, deep saucepan.
2. Sift together the bicarbonate of soda, cumin, flour and salt in a bowl.
3. Gradually add the water to make a batter. The consistency should be pliable, but not too dry or too runny.
4. Scoop out tablespoon-sized dumplings of batter and carefully lower into the hot oil.
5. Fry for around 3 minutes.
6. When the dumplings are done, remove them with a slotted spoon and place on a few sheets of kitchen paper to drain off excess oil.
7. To make the yoghurt sauce, melt the butter or ghee in a heavy-based pan, then add the onion, ginger, cumin, cinnamon, cloves and cardamom. Stir over a medium heat for about 3 minutes until the onions have softened.
8. Add the chickpea flour and continue stirring for another 2 minutes.
9. Remove from the heat and stir in the water and yoghurt. Increase the heat, then return the pan to the stove and stir until the sauce thickens.
10. Divide the dumplings among four bowls and coat with the yoghurt sauce. Sprinkle with the basil, mint and chilli and serve.

Sage

What's in a name?

Sage got its present-day name from the Latin *salvia*, meaning 'healing plant'.

Historical notes

Sage was an important medicinal herb in the ancient world, and both the Greeks and Romans used it to cure a range of ailments, from diarrhoea to amnesia. During medieval times, the leaves were used to clean teeth and in the Victorian period it was often recommended as a cure for dandruff.

A few facts

- Sage is a hardy, evergreen herb of the mint family.
- There are hundreds of species, the most popular being the common sage that grows into a large bush with elongated purple-blue flowers and oval green leaves, a favourite in my herb garden.

Health & fitness

- An infusion made with sage leaves makes a good mouthwash, as they contain natural antiseptic.
- Sage helps with digestion, hence the reason it can so often be paired with fatty foods such as pork.
- If suffering from indigestion, it is recommended that sage be drunk as a tea.

Hints & tips

When picking sage, collect it first thing in the morning, before the sun hits its leaves. This will ensure a fresher, cleaner flavour with all the natural essential oils being intact.

Potato gnocchi
with sage butter
Serves 4–6

There are many ways to make gnocchi, but this is a recipe that works well with leftover potatoes if you have any. It is a cheap and filling dish, and Italian comfort food at its best.

300 g baking potatoes, baked, peeled
   and mashed

100 g white bread flour

1 egg

1 egg yolk

30 ml unsalted butter

salt and freshly ground black pepper

15 ml finely chopped fresh sage

30 ml chopped fresh flat-leaf parsley

50 ml double cream

125 g Parmesan cheese, grated

a little flour for dusting

Sage butter

120 g unsalted butter

30 ml finely chopped fresh sage

1 ml cayenne pepper

2.5 ml freshly ground black pepper

1. Mix the mashed potatoes in a bowl with the flour, egg, egg yolk and butter and mix well.
2. Add salt and pepper, sage, parsley, double cream and cheese, and mix well.
3. Mould into equal-sized balls (about walnut size).
4. Dust with a little flour and flatten slightly with the back of a fork
5. Place into gently simmering water and cook for 4–5 minutes.
6. Carefully remove with a slotted spoon and drain.
7. To make the sage butter, melt the butter gently over a low heat, then add all the remaining ingredients.
8. Cook gently over a very low heat for 3 minutes.
9. Pour the sage butter over the gnocchi and serve immediately.

hint

Add some tomato diamonds to give the sage butter a beautiful colour.

Savoury couscous

Serves 4

Couscous is quick, simple to make and inexpensive. It goes well with meat, fish and poultry and is a good substitute for potatoes. It can even be used as a stuffing.

20 ml butter

1 shallot or small onion, chopped

5 ml ground cinnamon

5 ml ground cumin

10 ml brown sugar

2.5 ml salt

175 g quick-cooking couscous

15 g sultanas

175 ml chicken stock

fresh coriander leaves

1. Melt the butter in a heavy-based pan and add the chopped shallot.
2. Add the cinnamon, cumin, sugar and salt and stir well.
3. Add the couscous and sultanas. Stir well.
4. Add the chicken stock and bring to the boil, stirring continuously.
5. Add the fresh coriander and cook for 2–3 minutes.
6. Remove from the heat and keep covered for 5 minutes before serving.

Quick stir-fried vegetables

Serves 4

For many years I have been pro-undercooking vegetables, possibly due to a throw-back as a child where the norm was to start boiling anything green or with a leaf at eight in the morning in readiness for lunch. I am pleased that my anarchistic approach years ago has now become the norm. Here my recipe incorporates a variety of shapes, textures and colours, all retaining a powerpack of nutrients and vitamins.

10 ml sesame oil

1 onion, finely sliced

2 cloves garlic, sliced lengthways

100 g broccoli florets

100 g mangetout

100 g baby sweetcorn, sliced diagonally

100 g fine beans

100 g spring onions, sliced lengthways

10 ml Thai fish sauce (nam pla) (optional)

20 ml soy sauce

1. Heat the oil until very hot, then carefully add the onion and garlic and immediately reduce the heat to medium.
2. Add the broccoli, mangetout, sweetcorn, beans and spring onions, and stir-fry quickly, leaving the vegetables firm and crisp to the bite.
3. Add the fish sauce, if using, then add the soy sauce.
4. Serve immediately, on its own or as an accompaniment to meat, fish or poultry.

5 minutes

Raspberry cranachan
Serves 4

A wee Scottish influence...and great if you're tight on time!

50 g rolled or fine oats, gently toasted
   in a dry pan for 2–3 minutes

75 ml malt whisky

15 ml clear honey

300 ml whipping cream

200–250 g cream cheese

700 g fresh or frozen raspberries

fresh mint leaves to decorate

1. Soak the warm toasted oatmeal in the whisky for a few minutes, and add the honey.
2. In a separate bowl, whisk the cream until double its volume, then fold in the cream cheese.
3. Fold the oatmeal and whisky mixture into the cream and cream cheese.
4. Spoon the cranachan into glasses, cover with the raspberries and decorate with fresh mint.

Gratin of frozen berries
with ginger sabayon
Serves 4

This dish, despite adding a lick of French with the words 'gratin' and 'sabayon', is very easy to make. I just couldn't bring myself to call it 'Grilled frozen fruits with ginger egg sauce'! Whichever way you say it, your guests will think it's magnifique.

500 g packet frozen mixed berries
   (e.g. strawberries, blackcurrants,
   redcurrants, blueberries, etc.)

Ginger sabayon

1 nugget preserved stem ginger

120 g castor sugar

4 medium egg yolks

15 ml preserving syrup

1. Preheat the grill.
2. Grate the preserved ginger and keep aside.
3. In a heatproof bowl suspended over a pan of boiling water, whisk together the sugar and egg yolks until light and fluffy.
4. Add the grated ginger and the preserving syrup and whisk to incorporate.
5. Arrange the frozen berries in the centre of each plate.
6. Spoon the sabayon over the berries, then place immediately under a very hot grill for 1–2 minutes only. Serve immediately.

Strawberry

What's in a name?

There are a couple of associations related to the strawberry. One probably comes from the Anglo-Saxon term for the wild strawberry plant, 'strawberries', meaning runners. The other relates to the bed of straw upon which the berries were cultivated to stop them coming into contact with the muddy earth.

Historical notes

The wild fruits were grown in ancient Rome and across Europe during the seventeenth century. The strawberries that we know today are relatively new fruits, and were developed when American species were brought together in the eighteenth century to produce the thousand or so varieties of cultivated strawberries around today.

A few facts

- The strawberry is a member of the rose family.
- It is the only fruit to have its pips on the outside.

Health & fitness

- Strawberries are a good source of Vitamin C and have the highest content of this vitamin than any other berry. Six strawberries contain as much Vitamin C as an orange.
- A 100 g portion of strawberries contains only 27 calories (113 kJ).
- In traditional medicine, they have long been used to cleanse and purify the digestive system, and are thought to act as a mild tonic for the liver and to have antibacterial properties.
- A book published in 1931 claimed that strawberries held on the teeth for 5 minutes would remove any discoloration, and a cut strawberry rubbed over the face after washing would whiten the skin and remove sunburn.

Hints & tips

- Always wash strawberries with their calyx still in place, as this prevents water entering into the centre of the fruit, which will thin down the flavour and wash away the nutrients.
- If strawberries lack flavour, dust them with icing sugar and keep aside for 45 minutes. Alternatively, sprinkle them with Kirsch, Cointreau or Grand Marnier liqueur.

Warm strawberry salad
with mint & pepper syrup
Serves 4

Fresh and healthy...a summer favourite.

95 g brown sugar

300 ml water

juice and grated zest of 1 lemon

15 ml freshly ground Sarawak (long) pepper (available from speciality food stores)

50 ml Cointreau, Grand Marnier or orange liqueur

550 g fresh strawberries, washed then hulled

50 g fresh mint, chopped

extra mint to decorate

1. Place the sugar and water into a saucepan and heat, stirring continuously until the sugar dissolves.
2. Bring the liquid to a simmer and add the lemon juice, zest and the ground pepper.
3. Remove from the heat, then add the liqueur and set aside.
4. Meanwhile, cut the strawberries in half or, if too large, into quarters, and place in a bowl. Pour over the pepper syrup.
5. Add the mint and stir gently.
6. Divide the mixture among four bowls, decorate with mint and serve.

Caramelized fruit salad
with spiced lime syrup

Serves 4

½ papaya (papaw), peeled, seeded and sliced

2 kiwi fruits, peeled and sliced

½ pineapple, peeled, cored and cut into small pieces

1 mango, peeled, stoned, and sliced

1 apple, peeled, cored and sliced

plain yoghurt for serving

Spiced lime syrup

2 fresh chillies

juice and zest of 2 limes

200 ml water

2 sticks cinnamon

150 g castor sugar

1. First make the syrup. Place all the syrup ingredients into a pan and bring to a gentle simmer, stirring until the sugar dissolves.
2. Simmer for 3–4 minutes, then remove from the heat.
3. Place all the prepared fruit into the hot syrup and leave to cool.
4. When cold, remove the cinnamon and chilli (or use as decoration), and serve the mixed fruit with a little of the syrup as well as a healthy dollop of yoghurt.

5 minutes

Quick and easy. Minimum cooking but maximum flavour, from hot and spicy, to fresh and fruity.

ten

10
minutes
cooking time

Chicken soup
Vietnamese-style
Serves 4

A quick, healthy soup – low in fat and very tasty.

175 g chicken breast fillets, skin removed, and thinly sliced

30 ml finely chopped garlic

1 medium onion, finely sliced

30 ml soy sauce

45 ml Thai fish sauce (nam pla)

1.2 litres chicken stock

1 small fresh Thai chilli, seeded and finely chopped

5 ml sugar

15 ml fresh lemon juice

450 g baby spinach, stalks removed and washed

30 ml rice wine vinegar (available from speciality and Asian food stores)

1. Combine the chicken, garlic, onion, 15 ml soy sauce and 15 ml fish sauce, then set aside to marinate.
2. Meanwhile, bring the chicken stock to a simmer, then add the chilli, sugar and lemon juice.
3. Bring back to a simmer, then add the chicken and a little of the marinade. Stir well.
4. Stir in the spinach.
5. Cook for 3–4 minutes, or until the chicken is cooked.
6. Remove from the heat and add the rice wine vinegar and remaining soy and fish sauces.
7. Divide among four bowls and serve hot.

Coconut & chicken broth
Thai-style
Serves 4

Simply delicious, and as hot as you want it!

Broth

700 ml chicken stock

60 g desiccated coconut

400 ml coconut milk

50 ml fresh cream

2 stalks lemon grass, bruised and
outer layer removed, thinly sliced

2 sticks celery, thinly sliced

2 small carrots, thinly sliced

1 onion, thinly sliced

zest of 1 lime

30 ml fresh lime juice

45 ml Thai fish sauce (nam pla)

Accompaniments

5 cm piece fresh root ginger, peeled
and thinly sliced

4 cloves garlic, thinly sliced

2 fresh Serrano chillies, seeded and
thinly sliced

1. Place all the broth ingredients into a saucepan and bring to a simmer.
2. Simmer for 7–8 minutes.
3. Remove from the heat and strain into warmed soup bowls.
4. Add a little of each accompaniment to each bowl and serve.

tips

- If you really want to go to town with this soup, try adding some poached slices of chicken or a few slices of fresh salmon.
- Udon noodles, coriander and bean sprouts also give this dish a stunning twist. However much time you wish to spend on it, simply enjoy!

10 minutes

Aubergine (brinjal) salad

Serves 4

3 medium young and fresh aubergines

45 ml lightly seasoned flour for dusting

90 ml olive oil

1 ml paprika

1 ml ground cumin

3 cloves garlic, crushed

sea salt and freshly ground black pepper

120 ml plain yoghurt

30 ml shredded fresh mint

sprigs of fresh mint to garnish

1. Cut the aubergines into 5 mm thick slices and dust with the seasoned flour.
2. Heat the olive oil until very hot, then sauté the aubergine slices until crisp on both sides.
3. Remove the slices with a slotted spoon and drain on kitchen paper. Dust with paprika and cumin.
4. In a clean bowl, mix together the garlic, salt, pepper, yoghurt and shredded mint.
5. Divide the aubergine slices among four plates, then drizzle the minted yoghurt over the slices.
6. Garnish with a sprig of fresh mint and serve.

Fresh mussels
with tomato & basil
Serves 4

A fresh, light and healthy lunch.

30 ml olive oil

4 shallots or small onions, finely sliced

2 cloves garlic, crushed

300 ml dry white wine

2 kg fresh black Knysna or green-lipped mussels, scrubbed and beards removed

560 g (about 5) medium vine-ripened tomatoes, quartered, or 560 g jar tomato purée (passata)

15 ml white wine vinegar

freshly ground black pepper

1 small bunch fresh basil

1. Heat the olive oil in a large, wide pan.
2. Add the shallots and the garlic, and cook slowly and gently for 2–3 minutes. Do not let them brown.
3. Add the white wine and bring to the boil.
4. Add the mussels, cover the pan, and cook for 3–4 minutes, stirring occasionally until the mussels have opened.
5. Remove the mussels with a slotted spoon and keep warm. (Discard any that do not open properly.)
6. Add the tomatoes, vinegar and pepper to the liquid in the pan and bring back to a simmer.
7. Return the mussels to the pan and stir them into the sauce.
8. Divide among four serving bowls and scatter fresh basil leaves over the top. Serve immediately.

10 minutes

Thai green chicken curry

Serves 4

30 ml sesame oil

30 ml Thai green curry paste

450 g chicken breast fillets, skin removed, and cut into finger-sized strips

2 cloves garlic, crushed

1 stalk lemon grass, bruised and outer layer removed

250 ml coconut milk

30 ml Thai fish sauce (nam pla)

45 ml sweet chilli sauce

1 fresh Thai green chilli, seeded and chopped

20 fresh basil leaves (preferably the purple variety), torn in half

1. Heat the sesame oil in a large frying pan.
2. Add the green curry paste and fry until bubbling.
3. Add the chicken, garlic and lemon grass, and fry for 3 minutes over high heat.
4. Add the coconut milk and bring rapidly to a simmer, stirring occasionally for about 5 minutes, or until the chicken is thoroughly cooked.
5. Stir in the fish sauce, sweet chilli sauce, green chilli and torn basil leaves.
6. Serve immediately with a little cooked rice.

10 minutes

Lamb

What's in a name?

The origin of the word 'lamb' is a difficult one to trace back as the name we use today derives from the Germanic word. The earliest records show that moufflon sheep were used mainly for their fleece. They were seldom used for food unless as part of a ritual sacrifice. The Romans called it *agnello*, the French *agneau*, so there are close similarities. The Germans call it *junges hammelfleish*, and there is also a story that the word lamb derived from the word used for llama, due to a small resemblance to this animal.

Historical notes

Roast sheep was the first sacrifice to the gods, and it is still associated with religious celebrations around the globe, such as Passover in the Jewish calendar, the Eid festival that marks the last month in the Muslim year, and Easter in the Christian churches.

A few facts

- Lamb is the meat of a young sheep slaughtered within one year of its birth. After a year, it could be called a hogget, old season lamb or even mutton, although mutton is usually associated with sheep of 3–4 years of age.
- Flavours that go well with lamb are, of course, mint, garlic and rosemary. Dried ginger can be rubbed into the meat prior to roasting, and orange is another flavour that complements lamb. In the Middle East, many lamb recipes contain cinnamon.

Health & fitness

- A 90 g serving of cooked lamb will supply about 20 g of protein (a third of our daily recommended amount). Lamb also provides Vitamin B and iron.
- Today lamb is bred to be leaner, but it still contains a high proportion of fat within the meat, although this depends greatly on the age, breed and the cut.

Hints & tips

Always bring refrigerated lamb back to room temperature before cooking, as it improves the browning and sealing of the meat.

Karoo lamb stir-fry
with bean sprouts & almonds
Serves 4

650 g lamb fillet or deboned rack
of lamb

10 ml cornflour

2 egg whites

15 ml soy sauce

5 ml freshly ground black pepper

45 ml groundnut (peanut) oil

3 cloves garlic, crushed

5 cm piece fresh root ginger, peeled
and finely chopped or grated

30 ml oyster sauce

45 ml dry sherry

5 ml demerara or light brown sugar

2 carrots, cut into thin batons

6 spring onions, shredded

250 g bean sprouts

30 ml flaked almonds, lightly toasted

1. Trim the lamb of any excess fat or sinew and slice thinly.
2. Mix together the cornflour, egg whites, soy sauce and pepper.
3. Add the lamb to this mixture and coat well.
4. Heat a wok or large frying pan, then add the oil, garlic and ginger. Sauté for 20–30 seconds to release the flavour.
5. Add the lamb and stir-fry for 3 minutes.
6. Add the oyster sauce, sherry and sugar and cook for about 2 minutes.
7. Add the carrots and spring onions and cook for another 2 minutes.
8. Finally, add the bean sprouts and cook for 1 minute.
9. Adjust seasoning, sprinkle the almonds over the top and serve immediately with Savoury Couscous (page 52) or Sweet-&-Sour Rice (page 100).

10 minutes

Indonesian beef satay
with beetroot chutney
Makes 10 snack bites or 4–6 lunchtime treats

Snack sticks, party bites or barbecue lunch.

soaked wooden skewers or
   metal skewers
a little oil (peanut, corn, sunflower
   or olive) for cooking
sour cream for serving

Beetroot chutney

450 g chopped onions
600 ml white wine vinegar
1 fresh red chilli, seeded and chopped
5 ml freshly ground black pepper
1.5 kg precooked beetroot, chopped
10 ml coarse sea salt
450 g Granny Smith apples, peeled,
   cored and chopped
450 g sugar

Beef satay

225 g lean beef mince
5 ml grated fresh root ginger
2 small cloves garlic, crushed
5 ml curry powder or paste
2.5 ml ground cumin
2.5 ml turmeric
30 ml desiccated or grated
   fresh coconut
15 ml Thai fish sauce (nam pla)
15 ml peanut butter
60 ml fresh white breadcrumbs

1. First make the chutney. Place the chopped onions into a pan with the vinegar, chilli and black pepper and bring rapidly to the boil.
2. Add the remaining ingredients and stir gently until the sugar has dissolved.
3. Bring back to a simmer and cook over medium heat until the chutney thickens. (If using precooked beetroot this will take around 10 minutes, if using fresh it will take about 45 minutes.)
4. Pour the chutney into hot, sterilized jars, leave to cool and store until ready to use.
5. To make the satays, mix together all the satay ingredients using clean hands. Make sure the mixture is well combined.
6. Divide the mixture into equal-sized balls (small ones for party bites, larger balls for a lunchtime meal).
7. Roll the meatballs into sausage shapes, then thread them onto the skewers, ensuring the meat is firm and tight. Brush with the oil.
8. Place under a hot grill, in a preheated oven at 180 °C, or on a barbecue, and cook, turning occasionally to cook through evenly. (The cooking time will depend on size and thickness – allow 5–6 minutes for the larger satays, or 3–4 minutes for the mini party size.)
9. When ready, serve with the beetroot chutney, a crisp green salad and a little sour cream.

10 minutes

Tamarind

What's in a name?

The name derives from the Latin *tamarindus*, and the Arabic *tamra Hindi*, meaning 'Indian date'.

Historical notes

The use of tamarind has been recorded as far back as 1298 AD, but it was possibly a native of East Africa. It is often associated with Hindu weddings, feasts and celebrations. In India, the whole of the tamarind plant is used, the fruit for seasoning and the flowers for vegetables.

A few facts

- Tamarind is the fruit of a tree and is shaped like a runner bean. It has a pale and brittle outer case that holds a dark brown, sticky pulp. Tamarind is normally used as a spice, but it is actually classed as a legume and belongs to the peanut family.
- Tamarind has a high tartaric acid content, which gives it its characteristic sour, but fruity and refreshing, flavour.

Health & fitness

- Tamarind is rich in vitamins and good for the liver and kidneys.
- In India, it is used as a remedy against dysentery and stomach upsets.
- Tamarind water makes a good gargle for sore throats.

Hints & tips

- If you cannot find tamarind for a recipe, substitute fresh lime.
- When buying a block of tamarind, choose one that is pliable and not hard.
- If using fresh tamarind and you need to strain the liquid, use a nylon sieve, as a metal one will react with the tartaric acid.

fifteen

This section is what I call midweek cooking. Had a busy day? Need something fairly quickly, nutritious and tasty? Then try the recipes on the pages that follow.

15 minutes
cooking time

cherry

What's in a name?

The word 'cherry' evolved from the medieval Latin *ceresia*, which eventually became *cerise* in French. The English dropped the '-se' at the end due to it sounding plural, and ended up calling it 'ceri'.

Historical notes

Cherries were first distributed through Europe by the Romans in 100 AD. The Roman general and bon viveur Lucullus brought the cherry tree from the city of Cerasus. The type of cherries known then, however, would have been the sour varieties and would have been used mainly for medicinal purposes.

A few facts

- There are more than 1 000 varieties of cherries, which are divided into two groups, the sour cherries, such as morello, and the sweet cherries, such as Napoleon and Bing.
- The sour varieties are usually dried or bottled, while the sweet varieties are usually reserved for eating fresh.
- In French cookery, any game, poultry or sweet dish with the word *montmorency* in its name, has a sauce of sour cherries.

Health & fitness

- Raw cherries are a good source of potassium, which helps to regulate the heartbeat as well as keep the skin healthy. They also contain a good amount of Vitamin C.
- In alternative medicine, cherries are used to help cure joint inflammation, and gout in particular, by helping to lower levels of uric acid in the blood.
- It is also believed that cherries have a cleansing effect and are able to remove toxins and cleanse the kidneys.

Hints & tips

When buying fresh cherries, check the stalks. They should be green and pliable; as they age the stalks dry and wither.

Cherry wine soup

Serves 4

This soup also makes a refreshing cocktail if you add chilled sparkling wine – delicious!

150 ml red wine

100 g castor sugar

500 g tinned morello cherries, juice
drained off

30 ml Maraschino (cherry) liqueur

200 ml fresh orange juice

100 ml water

1 stick cinnamon

1. In a heavy-based pan, heat the wine and castor sugar,
    stirring until the sugar is dissolved.
2. Add the remaining ingredients and bring to a simmer.
3. Cook gently for 6–7 minutes, then remove from the
    heat and keep aside to cool slightly. Remove cinnamon.
4. Blitz with a hand-held blender until smooth.
5. Divide the soup among four bowls and serve warm.
    Alternatively, chill and serve in glasses with a swirl of
    cream and a sprig of mint.

Hearty butter bean soup

Serves 4

5 ml cumin seeds

5 ml crushed coriander seeds

25 ml olive oil

1 onion, chopped

2 cloves garlic, crushed

1 leek, white part only, chopped

1 fresh green chilli, seeded and
chopped

1 carrot, finely chopped

4 rashers rindless bacon, chopped

400 g tin butter beans, drained
and rinsed

1.2 litres chicken stock

salt and freshly ground black pepper

crème fraîche and parsley to garnish

1. Heat a large, heavy-based pan and dry-fry the cumin
    and coriander seeds.
2. Remove the seeds from the pan and crush them in a
    pestle and mortar until they form a fine powder.
3. In the same pan, heat the olive oil, then add the onion,
    garlic and leek, and let them sweat.
4. Add the chilli and carrot, then the bacon and ground
    spices, and cook for 1–2 minutes.
5. Add the butter beans and stock, and bring to the boil.
6. Simmer for 10–12 minutes.
7. Season to taste, then purée the soup in a food
    processor or push it through a sieve.
8. Reheat and serve with a swirl of crème fraîche and
    some parsley.

Prawn gaeng som

Serves 4

Prawn paste

5 large dried red chillies

10 shallots or 3 small onions, chopped

5 cm piece fresh root ginger, peeled and grated

50 g raw prawns (or shrimps)

2 cloves garlic, crushed

Soup

1.2 litres water or chicken stock

6 button mushrooms, washed and thinly sliced

1 courgette (baby marrow), cut into thin batons

8 large fresh prawn tails, deveined

5 ml castor or palm sugar

30 ml Thai fish sauce (nam pla)

juice of 1 lime

50 g fresh coriander leaves

1. To make the prawn paste, place all the paste ingredients in a food processor and blend until smooth. Keep aside.
2. To make the soup, heat the water or stock in a large pan until it comes to a simmer, then add the mushrooms and courgette. Stir in the prawn paste and simmer for 8–10 minutes.
3. Add the prawn tails and simmer for a further 3 minutes, or until cooked through. Switch off the heat, but do not remove it from the stove.
4. Before serving, add the sugar, fish sauce and lime juice and stir.
5. Ladle the soup into bowls and scatter with the coriander.

Seafood frittata
with fresh tomato salsa

Serves 4

This is a great dish for a quick lunch and a great way to liven up ready-cooked potatoes!

60 g unsalted butter

16 thin slices cooked potato

6 medium eggs

45 ml crème fraîche

150 ml double cream

10 ml horseradish sauce

25 g snipped fresh chives

25 g chopped fresh flat-leaf parsley

30 ml drained capers

zest and juice of ½ lemon

salt and freshly ground black pepper

450 g mixed fresh or frozen seafood
of choice (cooked mussels,
prawns, raw salmon, flakes
of smoked mackerel, tuna,
snoek, etc.)

55 g fresh white breadcrumbs

Fresh tomato salsa

2 vine-ripened tomatoes, peeled,
seeded and chopped

2 spring onions, finely sliced

30 ml chopped fresh coriander

2 jalapeno chillies, seeded
and chopped

salt and freshly ground black pepper

1 ml brown sugar

2.5 ml white wine vinegar

1. Preheat the oven to 180 °C.
2. Place the butter in a large, non-stick, ovenproof pan and melt over a gentle heat.
3. Place a layer of potato on the base of the pan and cook gently.
4. Meanwhile, mix together the eggs, crème fraîche and double cream.
5. Add the horseradish, chives, parsley, capers, lemon zest and juice, salt and pepper and stir well.
6. Add the seafood to the egg mixture, then pour it over the potatoes. Sprinkle with the breadcrumbs.
7. Place in the oven for 12–13 minutes until set.
8. When ready, remove from the oven and turn out onto a serving plate.
9. To make the salsa, simply mix all the salsa ingredients together.
10. Serve with the tomato salsa and a crisp salad drizzled with Lemon & Coriander Dressing (page 34).

Alan's quick curry

Hot and fragrant.

30 ml corn, peanut or olive oil

2 medium onions, cut into sixths

3 cloves garlic, sliced

15 ml hot curry powder

2 green chillies, finely chopped (with seeds)

2.5 ml paprika

10 ml cumin seeds

5 ml ground cinnamon

4 x 180 g chicken breast fillets, skin removed, chopped into 1.5 cm cubes

salt and freshly ground black pepper

2 tomatoes, chopped

15 ml tomato paste

25 ml water

75 ml coconut cream

zest and juice of 1 lime

1. Heat the oil in a large pan.
2. Add the onions and cook for 2–3 minutes.
3. Add the garlic, followed by the curry powder, chilli, paprika, cumin and cinnamon, and cook for a further 2 minutes until fragrant. Stir continuously.
4. Season the chicken breast pieces with salt and pepper and add to the hot spices in the pan. Stir well, making sure the chicken pieces are well coated with the spices.
5. Add the tomatoes, tomato paste and water and keep over a high heat for 3–4 minutes, stirring occasionally.
6. Add the coconut cream and bring back to a simmer. Cook for a further 2–3 minutes.
7. Finally add the lime juice and zest and stir well.
8. Serve with Sweet-&-Sour Rice (page 100).

15 minutes

Middle Eastern kibbeh

Serves 4

Kibbeh is a tasty Middle Eastern speciality of minced lamb and bulgur wheat, shaped into patties and fried. This dish is great for lunch or dinner and is ideal to take on a picnic.

450 g lamb mince (you can also use beef mince)

45 ml olive oil

1 onion, finely chopped

50 g pine nuts (you can also use hazelnuts or walnuts)

7.5 ml ground allspice

60 ml chopped fresh coriander

225 g bulgur wheat, soaked and drained

1 fresh red chilli

5 ml tomato paste

120 g mozzarella cheese, grated (optional)

15 ml finely chopped fresh rosemary

salt and freshly ground black pepper

a little oil for frying

1. With the exception of the mozzarella, rosemary, seasoning and oil for frying, place all the ingredients into a food processor and blitz until well combined.
2. Divide the kibbeh mixture into equal-sized balls – about the size of golf balls.
3. Using your thumb, make a hole in the centre and stuff it with some of the mozzarella and a sprinkling of chopped rosemary.
4. Close up the meatballs again and flatten them to form patties. Season lightly.
5. Heat the oil in a heavy-based frying pan, then carefully add the patties to the hot pan.
6. Fry for around 4 minutes on both sides or until cooked all the way through.
7. Serve immediately or chill for a picnic lunch. You can serve these with Chilli Dipping Sauce (page 21), Mint and Chilli Chutney (page 40), Quick Spring Onion Relish (page 112) or Chilli and Apple Chutney (page 136).

Grilled pork chops
with garlic & lime
Serves 4

An all-weather dish, where the marinade becomes the sauce.

4 x 240 g pork loin chops

6 cloves garlic, crushed

30 ml soy sauce

30 ml grated fresh root ginger

10 ml Dijon mustard

juice of 3 limes

15 ml sunflower oil

15 ml sesame oil

½ fresh chilli, seeded and finely chopped

1. Place all the ingredients, with the exception of the pork chops, into a plastic bag and mix well.
2. Add the pork chops and massage gently with the spices.
3. Preheat a grill or barbecue until very hot.
4. Remove the pork chops from the marinade and shake off any excess.
5. Place the chops on a grill tray or barbecue grill and cook for 4–5 minutes on each side.
6. While the chops are grilling, pour the leftover marinade into a pan and slowly bring to the boil. Simmer for 3–4 minutes.
7. When the chops are ready, drizzle the sauce over them and serve with a fresh crisp salad with Green Goddess Dressing (page 33) and/or creamy mashed potatoes.

15 minutes

cheese

What's in a name?

Cheese derives from the Latin *caseus*. The French word *fromage* derived from the word 'forma', the wicker basket in which the cheese was moulded.

Historical notes

- The discovery of cheese dates back 9 500 years, when nomads in the Middle East apparently discovered the first cheese-making process. The discovery was purely by chance, when milk that was being carried in sacks made from animal stomachs turned into curds. The natural enzyme (rennet) was still alive and kicking in the animal sack.
- All the ancient civilizations made cheese, and traces have even been found in an Egyptian tomb dating back to around 3 000 BC.

A few facts

- There are thousands of varieties of cheese, with over 800 varieties from France alone.
- Cheese is a product of curds, drained and often fermented. The milk of cows, goats and sheep are mostly used, partly skimmed or enriched with cream. Each cheese is made differently.
- On average, it takes 4.5 litres of milk to make approximately 500 g of cheese.

Health & fitness

- Cheese is a good source of protein and is rich in calcium. It is also an important source of Vitamine B12 for vegetarians.
- It is high in saturated fats and calories that are known to increase blood cholesterol. Some cheeses can contain six times more saturated fat than a sirloin steak.

Hints & tips

Chewing a piece of Cheddar cheese after a meal may help fight tooth decay, as it prevents the formation of acids in the mouth that can attack the enamel on teeth.

Gruyère fondue

Serves 4

It's back! The '70s party favourite returns.

400 g Gruyère cheese, grated

60 g Parmesan cheese, grated

30 g plain (cake) flour

10 ml mustard powder

250 ml dry white wine

30 ml crème fraîche or soured cream

5 ml freshly ground black pepper

1 ml grated nutmeg

1. In a bowl, combine the Gruyère and Parmesan cheeses, the flour and mustard powder.
2. In a heavy-based pan, heat the wine and add the cheese mixture, stirring continuously until melted.
3. Bring the mixture to a simmer, then reduce the heat.
4. Add the crème fraîche, pepper and nutmeg. Stir well.
5. To serve, just dip in pieces of day-old bread or toast, and enjoy.

15 minutes

99

Sweet-&-Sour rice

Serves 4–6

450 g jasmine rice

50 g butter

750 ml cold water or chicken
   or vegetable stock

100 ml plain yoghurt

15 ml clear honey

juice and zest of 1 lime

salt and freshly ground black pepper

1. Rinse the rice thoroughly to remove excess starch.
2. Melt the butter in a heavy-based saucepan. Add the rice and stir thoroughly, then add the water or stock and stir once.
3. Bring to the boil, uncovered, over medium heat. Reduce the heat and simmer for 12 minutes.
4. The rice is ready when all the water has been absorbed and evaporated. Remove from the heat, cover with a lid and leave to rest for a couple of minutes. Just before serving, add all the remaining ingredients and stir well. Serve.

Penne pasta
with spicy sausage & roast tomato cream

Serves 4

500 g penne pasta

75 ml olive oil

1 small onion, finely sliced

2 cloves garlic, crushed

750 g chorizo sausage, thinly sliced

10 ml finely chopped fresh rosemary

5 ml chopped fresh sage

1 fresh chilli, seeded and chopped

2 bay leaves

2 x 240 g tins plum tomatoes

30 ml castor sugar

25 ml balsamic vinegar

150 ml double cream or crème fraîche

grated Parmesan cheese for serving

1. Preheat the oven to 240 °C.
2. Cook the pasta for about 9 minutes in plenty of boiling salted water.
3. While the pasta is cooking, heat the olive oil in a large, ovenproof pan. Add the onion, garlic and sausage and cook gently for 2–3 minutes.
4. Add the rosemary, sage, chilli and bay leaves.
5. Add the tomatoes, sprinkle with castor sugar and balsamic vinegar, and then place in the oven to roast for 6–8 minutes.
6. Remove the pan from the oven and stir in the cream.
7. Drain the pasta and add the tomato cream to it. Stir well and serve with a little Parmesan cheese.

15 minutes

Fear-free chocolate soufflé

Serves 4

When faced with the thought of producing a soufflé for that all-important dinner party, the task can be quite daunting. Will it rise? Is it cooked all the way through? Will it fall flat? This recipe holds longer than other soufflés, tastes fantastic and is purposely meltingly saucy in the centre.

a little butter for greasing and cocoa
   powder for dusting
150 g good quality dark chocolate
   (preferably with 50 per cent
   cocoa solids)
25 ml unsalted butter
6 eggs, separated
35 ml castor sugar

1. Preheat the oven to 200 °C.
2. Liberally butter four 8.5 cm wide x 4 cm deep soufflé dishes and lightly dust with cocoa powder. Set aside.
3. Break the chocolate into small pieces and place in a clean heatproof bowl.
4. Add the butter and suspend the bowl over a pan of boiling water. When the butter and chocolate have melted – take care not to let it overheat – remove and set aside.
5. Place the egg yolks and 25 ml of the castor sugar in a separate heatproof bowl suspended over boiling water and whisk until thickened, pale and fluffy.
6. Pour the melted chocolate and butter mixture onto the fluffy eggs and fold it in carefully with a metal spoon.
7. In a separate bowl, whisk the egg whites with the remaining castor sugar until it forms stiff peaks, then, using a metal spoon, fold this carefully into the chocolate mix.
8. Pour the mixture into the prepared soufflé dishes until they are three-quarters full. Place on a baking sheet.
9. Place in the oven for 10–12 minutes until well risen and light.
10. When the soufflés are ready, remove them from the oven, dust with a little more cocoa powder and serve immediately.

hint

This soufflé works well with some fresh raspberries and/or vanilla ice cream on the side.

Dessert omelette
with cherry casserole
Serves 4

Light and fruity.

5 large eggs, separated

grated zest of ½ lemon

80 g plain (cake) flour, sifted

60 g butter, melted

100 g castor sugar

30 ml butter for frying

Cherry casserole

5 ml butter

250 g castor sugar

175 ml light and fruity red wine

juice of 1 orange

juice and zest of 1 lemon

450 g stoned cherries (fresh or
    tinned)

1 stick cinnamon

75 ml Pernod, Ricard or pastis

5 ml cornflour or arrowroot, diluted
    with a little red wine

1. Preheat the oven to 200 °C.
2. Mix together the egg yolks and lemon zest, then add the sifted flour and melted butter.
3. In a separate bowl, whisk together the egg whites and castor sugar as if making a meringue, until stiff peaks form.
4. Fold the whisked egg whites into the yolk mixture with a metal spoon, taking care to keep the mixture light and airy.
5. Melt the 30 ml butter in a large, non-stick, ovenproof frying pan, and swirl it around to ensure the sides of the pan are also lightly buttered.
6. Pour the mixture into the pan and level off with a wet palette knife or the back of a wet spoon.
7. Cook on top of the stove for about 2 minutes, then place the pan in the oven for 5–7 minutes.
8. While the omelette is in the oven, prepare the cherry casserole. Slowly melt the butter and castor sugar with the red wine, orange and lemon juice, stirring until all the sugar has dissolved.
9. Bring the liquid to a rapid boil, then add the cherries, zest, cinnamon and Pernod.
10. Cook for 3–4 minutes.
11. Add the dissolved cornflour and bring back to the boil, stirring continuously until the sauce has thickened. Remove cinnamon.
12. To serve, divide the omelette into the number of portions required and pour the cherry sauce over. You can also add a little double cream if desired.

twenty

This is a great selection of quick, easy dishes, and many of them work well for both indoor and outdoor cooking.

20.
minutes
cooking time

Smoked fish chowder
with poached hen's eggs
Serves 4

Great for a light lunch or dinner.

560 g smoked fish, cut into bite-sized pieces (e.g. haddock or smoked snoek)

500 ml fresh milk

1 medium onion, finely chopped

250 ml dry white wine

250 ml light fish stock or water

1 bay leaf

40 ml butter

60 ml plain (cake) flour

4 eggs

15 ml fresh lemon juice

salt and freshly ground black pepper

chopped fresh parsley to garnish

1. Place the smoked fish in the milk with the onion and wine, stock or water, and the bay leaf.
2. Bring to a gentle simmer and cook for 7–10 minutes.
3. While the fish is poaching, put some water on the boil for the eggs.
4. Melt the butter in a heavy-based pan.
5. Add the flour and stir for 2–3 minutes.
6. Gradually add the fish and poaching liquid (including the onion and bay leaf), stirring continuously until all the ingredients have been incorporated.
7. Break the four eggs into four cups.
8. When the water is boiling, switch off the heat and stir the water in a circular motion.
9. Add the eggs, one at a time, and leave to cook for 5–6 minutes.
10. Meanwhile, remove the bay leaf from the chowder and blitz the mixture until smooth.
11. Return the chowder to the pan to reheat and add the lemon juice and seasoning.
12. Ladle the chowder into four warm bowls and add the poached eggs.
13. Sprinkle with a little fresh parsley and serve immediately.

20 minutes

Crab

What's in a name?

The word 'crustacean' is derived from the Latin *crusta*, meaning shell or rind. 'Crab' comes from the old German *krabben*, meaning to claw.

Historical notes

Over the centuries, crabs have often been the food of the rich, rather than the poor. When Marco Polo visited China in the thirteenth century, he noted that prawns and crabs were turned into delicate little dim sum for the powerful elite, while the more common molluscs, such as oysters and mussels, were offloaded to the peasants.

A few facts

- There are more than 4 500 different species of crabs around the world. They range from tiny crabs that can live inside small shells and are no bigger than a fingernail, to huge spider crabs with a 3.5 m leg span.
- A crab must moult in order to grow, swelling up with water and shedding its old carapace. Each moult may add 2–5 cm in diameter.
- The meat from a crab makes up just 30–35 per cent of its total weight.

Health & fitness

Crabs and other shellfish are compact storehouses of vital nutrients. Most supply abundant Vitamin B13, which is necessary for the formation of red blood cells and to maintain a healthy nervous system. They also contain zinc, which is important for the production of proteins, speeds up the healing process and contributes to the development of the reproductive organs.

Hints & tips

When buying crabs, always pick them up and shake them. They should be heavy, but you should not feel or hear any liquid inside them. They are also best bought while they are alive, as they deteriorate quickly after death.

Oriental crab omelette
with chicken syrup

Serves 4

A lunch or dinner omelette with a twist.

Crab omelette

8 large eggs

salt and freshly ground black pepper

250 g white crab meat (fresh is best, but this recipe is flexible enough to use frozen or tinned)

60 g button mushrooms

1 small stick celery, washed

100 g fresh bean sprouts

1 small onion, roughly chopped

5 ml grated fresh root ginger

a little oil for cooking

Chicken syrup

15 ml cornflour

175 ml chicken stock

10 ml brown sugar

10 ml soy sauce

1. Preheat the grill.
2. Break the eggs into a large bowl and whisk with a little salt and pepper. Keep aside.
3. Place the remaining omelette ingredients, except the oil, into a food processor and give it a couple of blasts to form a coarse, chunky mixture.
4. Heat a square or rectangular non-stick baking or roasting tray (24 x 30 cm) with a little oil and pour in half the egg mixture. Place under the grill for 3–4 minutes.
5. When nearly cooked, evenly scatter over the crab filling, leaving a small area around the outsides free of the mixture.
6. Pour over the remaining egg and place back under the grill for another 3–4 minutes to finish cooking.
7. To make the chicken syrup, blend together the cornflour and a little of the cold stock.
8. Warm the remaining stock in a small saucepan and add the diluted cornflour, the sugar and soy sauce. Bring to the boil, stirring continuously for 3–4 minutes.
9. When ready, present the omelette by cutting it into shapes, squares or rounds and pile a couple of slices carefully on top of each other.
10. Pour the syrup over the omelette and serve with a crisp salad dressed with Alan's Summer Dressing (page 34).

Blackened chicken
with Cuban mojo

Serves 4

6 cloves garlic, roughly chopped

1 medium onion, chopped

10 ml cayenne pepper

5 ml paprika

2.5 ml ground allspice

5 ml freshly ground black pepper

5 ml chopped fresh thyme

4 x 180 g chicken breast fillets,
  skin removed

Mojo dressing

60 ml olive oil

6 cloves garlic, crushed

2.5 ml ground cumin

juice of 1–2 grapefruits (you need
  about 180 ml)

segments of 1 grapefruit

salt and freshly ground black pepper

1. Preheat the grill.
2. To prepare the chicken, place the garlic, onion, spices and thyme into a food processor and blitz until it forms a purée.
3. Using a thin-bladed knife, make 3–4 insertions in each chicken breast, but do not cut all the way through.
4. Rub the purée all over the chicken breasts.
5. When the grill is hot, place the chicken into a grill pan and place on the lower grill shelf.
6. Cook the chicken for 7–8 minutes on each side, or until cooked through.
7. Meanwhile, prepare the mojo dressing. Heat the olive oil in a saucepan over medium heat.
8. Add the garlic and cook for about 1 minute until fragrant – do not brown.
9. Add the cumin and mix in well.
10. Add the grapefruit juice and bring to a simmer for a couple of minutes.
11. Add the grapefruit segments and season to taste.
12. Serve the chicken with the hot or cold mojo dressing and Sweet-&-Sour Rice (page 100) or a fresh salad.

20 minutes

110

Skewered turkey
with quick spring onion relish

Serves 4

450 g turkey breast

300 ml plain yoghurt

5 ml paprika

grated zest and juice of 1 lemon

10 ml turmeric

salt and freshly ground black pepper

4 soaked wooden skewers or
   metal skewers

Quick spring onion relish

45 ml sesame seeds

1 bunch spring onions, chopped

10 ml grated fresh root ginger

22.5 ml light soy sauce

10 ml rice wine vinegar or dry sherry

15 ml sesame oil

5 ml clear honey

1. Cut the turkey breast into bite-sized portions and place in a bowl.
2. Add the remaining ingredients to the turkey pieces and mix together.
3. Thread the turkey pieces neatly onto the skewers.
4. Heat an oiled griddle pan (or place over coals on a barbecue) and cook for around 8–10 minutes.
5. To make the relish, place all the relish ingredients into the food processor and blend until it forms a coarse pulp.
6. Serve the turkey skewers with the spring onion relish, a bowl of potato salad and a fresh green salad.

Lamb koftas
in yoghurt sauce

Serves 4

oil for deep-frying

500 g lamb mince

1 small egg

2.5 ml garam masala

15 ml cornflour

15 ml plain (cake) flour

Yoghurt sauce

60 g butter

1 medium onion, sliced

5 ml grated fresh root ginger

1 fresh chilli, seeded and finely
chopped

2.5 ml ground cumin

2.5 ml ground cinnamon

1 ml ground cloves

2.5 ml ground cardamom

50 g chickpea flour

150 ml water

250 ml plain yoghurt

30 ml chopped fresh basil

15 ml chopped fresh mint

1. Heat the oil for deep-frying.
2. Mix together the mince, egg, garam masala and cornflour until smooth and well blended.
3. Roll heaped teaspoons of the mixture into oval shapes and toss in the flour.
4. Deep-fry the koftas in batches for around 2 minutes or until golden brown.
5. While the koftas are frying, make the yoghurt sauce. Melt the butter in a heavy-based pan and add the onion, ginger, chilli, cumin, cinnamon, cloves and cardamom. Stir over a medium heat for about 3 minutes until the onion has softened.
6. Add the chickpea flour and stir over a medium heat for 2 minutes. Remove from heat.
7. Stir in the water and yoghurt, and return to the heat until the sauce thickens.
8. When the koftas are ready, remove them with a slotted spoon and drain on kitchen paper. Place them into the yoghurt sauce and cook through for 5 minutes.
9. To serve, place equal quantities of koftas onto serving plates, spoon over some sauce and sprinkle with the chopped basil and mint.

Perfect burgers

Makes 8 burgers

45 ml vegetable oil

1 large onion, finely chopped

1 kg quality mature minced beef steak (not extra lean)

20 ml English mustard powder

20 ml horseradish sauce

60 ml soured cream

30 ml chopped fresh flat-leaf parsley

3 eggs, lightly beaten

sea salt and freshly ground black pepper

burger buns, ketchup and salad for serving

1. Heat 15 ml of the oil in a small frying pan with a lid, and gently fry the onion for 4–5 minutes until softened but not coloured. Remove from the heat and leave to cool.
2. Place the mince in a large bowl. Add the cooled onion and all the other ingredients, except the remaining oil, season well and mix to combine.
3. Divide and shape the mixture into 8 x 2.5 cm thick burgers. Refrigerate until needed.
4. Brush a medium-hot griddle pan or barbecue with a little of the remaining oil before cooking the burgers for about 5–6 minutes on each side, or until cooked through.
5. Serve in lightly toasted burger buns, with ketchup and salad.

20 minutes

Pork saltimbocca
with honey-mustard dressing
Serves 4

A classic that is back in fashion, easy to prepare, and wonderful to eat. The translation of the Italian name, saltimbocca, means 'jump into your mouth'. You will be pleased they do!

4 x 175 g pork slices taken from the fillet or loin, cut about 5 mm thick

salt and freshly ground black pepper

16 large fresh sage leaves

4 slices Parma ham or bacon

60 g unsalted butter

juice of 1 lemon

2.5 ml paprika

1. Place the pork slices between sheets of clingfilm and batten out lightly to about 4 mm thick. Season with salt and black pepper.
2. Place a sage leaf on top of the pork, then roll it up and wrap the Parma ham or bacon around. Secure with a toothpick.
3. Place half the butter into a heavy-based frying pan over a high heat.
4. When the butter has melted, add the pork and cook for 2–3 minutes on each side, crisping the Parma ham and cooking until golden.
5. Remove the toothpicks and cook on a more gentle heat for an additional 5 minutes, turning occasionally throughout the cooking period.
6. Meanwhile, finely chop the remaining sage and add it to the lemon juice.
7. When the pork is ready, turn the heat back up to high and pour over the lemon juice. Add the remaining butter and paprika.
8. Roll the pork around in the juices to coat, flavour and colour the meat.
9. Serve immediately with a crisp salad, a drizzle of Honey-Mustard Dressing (page 34) and Sweet-&-Sour Rice (page 100).

20 minutes

Onion

What's in a name?

It is thought that the word 'onion' comes from the Latin *unio*, meaning single pearl, a name that ancient farmers gave their pick of the crop. This may also explain the origin of the phrase 'knowing your onions', which means to be very knowledgeable about a product.

Historical notes

- In 1750 BC the laws of Hammarobi (which evolved into Mesopotamia) ruled that the poor and needy be provided with a monthly ration of bread and onions.
- For the poor of ancient Rome, onions were part of their staple diet and were often eaten raw, as we would eat an apple today.
- In ancient Egypt, onions were used to decorate the eye sockets of Egyptian mummies, and during the Middle Ages they were used as a charm against the plague.

A few facts

- There are over 500 varieties of onions. The most widely used is the common onion (*Allium cepa*). Onions range in size from tiny pearls to the size of a small melon. They also vary in colour from brown, yellow and white to red. In taste, and as a general rule of thumb, the brown skins can be slightly bitter, while the red and white varieties are milder and sweeter.
- The onion's relatives include leeks, chives, spring onions and garlic.

Health & fitness

- In ancient Egypt, Greece and Rome, onions were used to treat heart problems and disease.
- Onions have been used as an antiseptic. The syrup was a remedy for coughs and colds, while raw onion was used for cuts and acne. It was even thought to make hair grow and clear sinus problems.
- Today, scientists agree that onions hold beneficial healing properties that may help to reduce cholesterol levels and even help prevent blood clotting.

Hints & tips

If cutting onions makes you cry, place the peeled onion into the freezer for 10–12 minutes. This will chill and weigh down the airborne vapours that usually head for the eyes and nose.

Caramelized red onion
& goat's cheese tart

Serves 4–6

25 ml peri-peri oil

3 red onions, finely sliced

2 cloves garlic, crushed

5 ml fresh thyme leaves

5 ml clear honey

12.5 ml chilli jam

6 x 1 cm thick slices goat's
  cheese log

150 ml fresh cream

2 eggs

salt and freshly ground black pepper

12.5 ml grated Parmesan cheese

No-roll buttermilk pastry

120 g self-raising flour

5 ml baking powder

2.5 ml cayenne pepper

pinch of salt

12.5 ml grated Parmesan cheese

75 ml buttermilk

25 ml sunflower oil

1. Preheat the oven to 180 °C.
2. To make the caramelized onions, heat the peri-peri oil in a heavy-based pan.
3. Add the sliced onions, garlic and thyme and stir gently for 2–3 minutes.
4. Reduce the heat and cover with a lid. Cook gently for 5–8 minutes.
5. Add the honey and chilli jam, stir and replace the lid, cooking over very low heat for a further 4–5 minutes.
6. When the onions are ready, switch off the heat and leave to cool.
7. For the buttermilk pastry, sift the flour, baking powder, cayenne pepper and salt into a bowl.
8. Add the Parmesan and make a well in the centre.
9. Pour in the buttermilk and sunflower oil and mix lightly, bringing together the ingredients to form a dough. Take care not to overmix.
10. Lightly oil a 10 x 30 cm rectangular tin (shape optional), or four 12 cm tins, and neatly line with the pastry, pressing it down. Refrigerate for 15 minutes.
11. To assemble the tart, spread a layer of onions over the pastry base, then top with a layer of goat's cheese.
12. Beat together the cream and eggs, and add salt and pepper, then pour this mixture over the goat's cheese and onions.
13. Sprinkle the Parmesan cheese over and place the tart into the oven for 7–9 minutes if using a convection oven, or 11–12 minutes if using a conventional oven. The tart is cooked when the egg mix is firm to the touch and the goat's cheese is golden brown on top.
14. Serve warm with a dressed salad.

20 minutes

118

Simple mashed potatoes
scented with nutmeg
Serves 4

900 g floury potatoes, peeled and
    quartered
100 g unsalted butter
120 ml double cream
salt and freshly ground black pepper
1 ml grated nutmeg

1. Boil the potatoes in salted water until tender – this should take 16–20 minutes, depending on size.
2. Drain off all the water and cover with a lid. Return to a very low heat and shake the pan vigorously for 2 minutes (this will start to break up the potatoes and remove any excess moisture, making them lighter and fluffier).
3. Mash the potatoes by hand.
4. Add the butter and cream a little at a time and finally, mash in the salt, pepper and nutmeg.

Pan haggerty potatoes
Serves 4

The name was originally one word – panhaggerty – meaning onions and potatoes.

450 g potatoes, peeled
50 g unsalted butter
250 g onions, finely chopped
salt and freshly ground black pepper
15 ml crème fraîche
125 g Cheddar cheese, grated
5 ml crushed caraway seeds

1. Preheat the oven to 180 °C.
2. Grate the potatoes, place in a clean tea towel, and squeeze out the starch liquid until dry. Do not wash.
3. Melt half the butter in an ovenproof heavy-based pan and the other half in a frying pan.
4. Add the onions to the frying pan and sweat off until translucent.
5. Add the potatoes to the ovenproof pan and press to form a solid mass that is evenly distributed in the pan.
6. Spoon the cooked onions on top of the potatoes and add seasoning.
7. Top with a little crème fraîche, sprinkle over the grated cheese and caraway seeds, then place in the oven to cook for 18–20 minutes.

20 minutes

120

Coconut

What's in a name?

The coconut got its name from the Spaniards, who thought that it had a similar appearance to that of a monkey's face – with two round eyes and a nose. *Coco* is the Spanish word for monkey, the nut part was added later.

Historical notes

- In the thirteenth century, Marco Polo came across the coconut during his travels in Indonesia. The Spanish and Portuguese introduced it to Central and South America during the sixteenth century.
- The inhabitants of the tropics called it the tree of life and it was hugely popular as every part of the nut was used: the flesh for food, the milk for drinking, the outer skin for bowls and water pipes, and the outer fibre for ropes and fishing nets.

A few facts

- The coconut palm grows faster than any other species of palm and can reach a height of 30 m. It bears 15–20 nuts that take a little more than a year to ripen from flower.
- A fresh coconut can be kept for up to a month at room temperature before opening.
- More people die each year from being hit by falling coconuts, than from shark attacks.

Health & fitness

Coconuts are a useful source of fibre. They do, however, contain 351 calories (1 469 kJ) per 100 g and are high in saturated fat, more than even the fattiest piece of meat. So avoid those creamy curries if you're watching your weight!

Hints & tips

To open a coconut, you need to focus on the centre of the nut, where it has a natural fault line. Hold the nut carefully and, using a hammer, hit it once, dead-centre, with a firm blow. The coconut should crack. Good luck!

Oriental poached dumplings
in coconut broth

Serves 4

Turn leftover potatoes into a comforting winter dessert.

Dumplings

225 g cooked potatoes (baked
    potatoes work best) or leftover
    mashed potatoes

35 g semolina

60 g butter, melted

1 ml salt

1 egg yolk

50 g self-raising flour

25 g fresh white breadcrumbs

1 ml ground cinnamon

30 g desiccated coconut

toasted coconut curls to decorate

Coconut broth

400 ml coconut milk

50 ml fresh cream

2.5 ml grated nutmeg

85 g castor sugar

2.5 ml ground allspice

50 ml water

1. If using baked potatoes, spoon the cooked potatoes out of their skins and mash, or pass through a potato ricer into a clean bowl.
2. Add the remaining dumpling ingredients and mix thoroughly by hand to form a smooth dough.
3. Wrap in clingfilm and refrigerate for a few minutes.
4. Meanwhile, prepare the coconut broth. Place all the broth ingredients into a heavy-based pan and heat gently, stirring continuously until the sugar has dissolved.
5. Bring to a simmer.
6. Remove the dumpling dough from the refrigerator and roll into thin sausage shapes on a lightly floured surface.
7. Remove small pieces of the dumpling mix and roll with lightly floured hands into a ball about the size of a small pebble or pea. Keep aside.
8. When all the dumplings are ready, place them in the coconut broth and simmer gently for 12–13 minutes.
9. When the dumplings float to the surface and are cooked, serve them in the broth in warmed bowls.
10. Sprinkle over toasted coconut curls to decorate.

20 minutes 123

Roast plums
in rosé wine

Serves 4

900 g firm fresh plums, washed and stoned

400 ml rosé wine

45 ml clear honey

juice and zest of 1 small orange

1 stick cinnamon

1. Preheat the oven to 180 °C.
2. Place the plums in a shallow earthenware dish and cover with the wine, honey, orange juice and zest. Add the cinnamon.
3. Bake in the oven for 20 minutes.
4. Remove from the oven and leave to cool.
5. Chill in the refrigerator for 10–15 minutes and serve with ice cream, plain yoghurt or crème fraîche, or use as a base for crumbles.

20 minutes

A great mix of family-style meals and dinner party dishes that will make people think you have been cooking for hours!

twenty-five

25
minutes
cooking time

Pea

What's in a name?

The word 'pea' derives from the Greek *pison*, meaning vegetable. It has only been called a pea from around the 1600s; prior to that they were called pise or pease (hence pease pudding).

Historical notes

- Peas have been eaten since neolithic times. Dried peas were the most common form and were used in soups, which sustained peasants in early medieval times in Europe and Asia, especially at the time of year when food was in short supply and fresh ingredients were non-existent.
- The Romans reputedly ate them like popcorn, probably while watching a gladiator fight, and in the French and Italian courts they were eaten as a snack.

A few facts

Frozen peas are probably one of the only vegetables that are better for you frozen than fresh. The reason for this is that as soon as the pods are harvested, the natural sugar in the peas begins to be converted into starch. As freezing usually takes place very soon after the pods have been picked, the chemical changes are minimal, whereas the fresh peas may take several days to reach the green-grocer or supermarket, by which time more of the sugar has turned into starch, losing sweetness, freshness and vitamins.

Health & fitness

- Peas are a rich source of vitamins B and C (especially if frozen) and contain protein, fibre, folate and phosphorus.
- One 65 g serving of cooked peas provides about 50 calories (209 kJ), plus a quarter of the Vitamin C and half the Vitamin B daily requirement.

Hint & tips

- Other than for soups, always cook peas for as short a time as possible, keeping them crisp and fresh and ensuring the flavour is fuller and sweeter.
- Peas are also extremely adaptable when marrying with other ingredients, ranging from mint, lettuce and smoky bacon to balsamic vinegar.

Pea pod soup
with flash-fried prawns & mint dressing
Serves 4

This soup makes a great dinner appetiser or light lunch.

Pea pod soup

50 g butter

50 g onion, chopped

2 rashers rindless bacon, chopped

50 g plain (cake) flour

100 ml milk

450 g shelled fresh or frozen peas

100 g pea pods or mangetout,
 roughly chopped

550 ml chicken stock

10 fresh mint leaves

60 ml double cream

salt and freshly ground black pepper

Flash-fried prawns

50 g butter

180 g prawn tails, peeled

juice of ½ lemon

salt and freshly ground black pepper

Mint dressing

24 fresh mint leaves, shredded

60 ml balsamic vinegar

90 ml extra virgin olive oil

salt and freshly ground black pepper

1. To make the soup, melt the butter in a heavy-based pan.
2. Add the onion and bacon and cook gently for 3–4 minutes.
3. Add the flour, stir well and cook for a further 1–2 minutes.
4. Add the milk, a little at a time, stirring continuously until all the milk has been used.
5. Add the peas, pea pods or mangetout, stir, then add the stock and mint.
6. Bring to the boil, then simmer, covered, for 15–20 minutes.
7. When ready, cool slightly and place in a food processor (or use a hand-held blender) and purée.
8. Return to the pan to reheat, then add the cream and season to taste.
9. To prepare the prawns, heat a pan and add the butter.
10. Once hot and foaming, add the prawns and quickly fry.
11. Pour over the lemon juice and season.
12. Place all the dressing ingredients into a bowl and stir until the sugar has dissolved.
13. To serve, ladle the soup into warmed bowls, add the flash-fried prawns and drizzle over the mint dressing. Serve immediately.

Red-skinned potato salad
with lager dressing
Serves 4

Here's a salad for the boys, and girls, of course.

4 medium red-skinned potatoes, washed (do not peel)
1 small red onion, finely chopped
30 ml finely chopped fresh flat-leaf parsley

Lager dressing
100 ml extra virgin olive oil
1 small onion, finely chopped
200 ml lager
22.5 ml cider vinegar or verjuice
5 ml castor sugar
15 ml Dijon mustard
sea salt and freshly ground black pepper

1. Cook the potatoes in boiling salted water for 20–25 minutes until tender. Drain and leave to cool slightly.
2. While the potatoes are cooking, make the lager dressing. Heat 30 ml of the olive oil in a small pan and gently fry the onion for about 5 minutes until softened but not catching colour.
3. Add the lager, cider vinegar and castor sugar and simmer for 5 minutes.
4. Pour this mixture into a food processor and add the mustard and seasoning. While the motor is running, slowly pour in the remaining oil to make a fairly thick dressing.
5. Slice the potatoes into 5 mm thick rounds, being careful not to break the skin too much.
6. While the potatoes are still warm, gently mix them with the lager dressing, chopped red onion and parsley, being careful not to break up the potatoes too much. Check seasoning.
7. Serve warm or at room temperature.

25 minutes

130

Butterfish
with basil, bacon & spring onion
Serves 4

Versatile and tasty, this dish also works well with other fish such as cod or salmon.

4 x 175 g fresh butterfish fillets

75 ml dry white wine

salt and freshly ground black pepper

15 ml unsalted butter

6 spring onions, finely sliced

30 ml small capers

225 ml full-fat crème fraîche

juice of ½ lemon

30 ml chopped fresh basil

15 ml finely chopped fresh parsley

4 rashers rindless bacon, cut into strips and grilled until crispy

caper berries to garnish

1. Place the fish into a pan, add the white wine, season with a little salt and pepper then dot with the butter.
2. Cover the pan with a lid, bring to a simmer and cook for 8–10 minutes. When cooked, remove the fish (keep the poaching liquid in the pan) and keep warm.
3. Meanwhile, turn up the heat and bring the poaching liquid to the boil, then reduce it to 30–45 ml.
4. Stir in the spring onions, capers and crème fraîche and bring back to a simmer. Add the lemon juice and stir well.
5. Add the basil and parsley and stir.
6. To serve, plate the fish, then pour over the sauce. Place the crispy bacon on the top of the fish and scatter with a little chopped basil and caper berries. Serve with a crisp salad, sweet potatoes or couscous.

25 minutes

Javanese-style chicken

Serves 4

4 x 240 g chicken breasts

10 ml ground coriander

10 ml ground cumin

10 ml ground cloves

10 ml turmeric

2 shallots or small onions, finely
chopped

2 fresh red chillies, seeded and finely
chopped

30 ml fresh lemon juice

120 g brown sugar

60 ml vegetable oil

salt and freshly ground black pepper

1. Preheat the oven to 200 °C.
2. Using a small sharp knife, make four small incisions across the chicken breasts.
3. Place the spices, shallots, chillies, lemon juice, sugar and 30 ml oil into a bowl and mix well. Massage this mixture into the breasts and incisions.
4. Oil a tray or roasting pan with the remaining oil and add the chicken.
5. Season with salt and pepper.
6. Place in the oven and cook for 18–20 minutes, or until cooked through.
7. When ready, serve with a fresh salad, dressing of choice (pages 33–34) and Quick Spring Onion Relish (page 112).

25 minutes

Grilled lamb
with chilli & apple chutney

Serves 4

700 g lamb fillet

Marinade

30 ml whole grain mustard

30 ml olive oil

1 large clove garlic, crushed

10 ml chopped fresh rosemary

5 ml soy sauce

Chilli and apple chutney

30 ml olive oil

1 small onion, finely chopped

2 dessert apples, peeled, cored
   and sliced

1 fresh red chilli, seeded and finely
   chopped

30 ml white wine vinegar

5 ml castor sugar

45 ml apple juice

30 ml chopped fresh coriander

1. Preheat the grill to very high.
2. Mix together all the marinade ingredients until they are well combined.
3. Add the lamb and thoroughly coat it in the marinade. Keep aside while making the chutney.
4. To make the chutney, heat the oil in a frying pan, add the onion and cook over a medium heat for 5 minutes until golden.
5. Add the apples, chilli, vinegar, sugar and apple juice.
6. Stir and leave to simmer for 5 minutes.
7. Add the coriander, remove from the heat and keep to one side.
8. Remove the lamb from the marinade, allow the excess to run off, and place the lamb on the grill rack.
9. Grill for 10–15 minutes, turning frequently until cooked through.
10. Serve slices with a crisp salad, Red-skinned Potato Salad with Lager Dressing (page 130) and a dollop of the chilli and apple chutney.

Jerk mince burgers

Serves 4

Jamaica is famous for its jerk dishes, in particular the jerk chicken, where pieces of dried chicken are slowly cooked in a blend of spices and Jamaican pepper. I have simplified the whole process and created an ideal blend of Caribbean flavour with an American burger.

900 g beef mince

2 egg yolks

85 g fresh brown breadcrumbs

10 spring onions, minced

2 fresh hot chillies, seeded and finely chopped

4 cloves garlic, crushed

5 ml ground cinnamon

10 ml ground allspice

salt and freshly ground black pepper

10 ml brown sugar

60 ml olive oil

4 bay leaves

crème fraîche or plain yoghurt for serving

1. Prepare the coals in the barbecue or preheat the oven to 180 °C.
2. Mix together all the ingredients, with the exception of the bay leaves and oil, in a large bowl.
3. Mould the mixture into four neatly shaped burgers, about 9 cm in diameter and 2.5 cm thick.
4. Cut four large squares of kitchen foil and brush thoroughly with the olive oil.
5. Place a burger in the centre of each foil square and top with a bay leaf.
6. Fold over the foil to form an envelope, ensuring that the burger is well sealed and protected. It may be good to wrap it in two layers of foil.
7. Place the parcels onto a hot barbecue or into the oven and cook for 12–15 minutes. If barbecuing, the cooking time will depend upon the heat of the coals.
8. When ready, open the parcels and remove the burgers.
9. Top with a dollop of crème fraîche or yoghurt and serve with the Warm Banana and Red Onion Salad (page 39).

25 minutes

Chilli

What's in a name?

The word 'chilli' comes from the term used for this plant by the early inhabitants of Mexico.

Historical notes

Chillies are natives of tropical America, where they were regularly used by the Aztecs and have even been found in Inca remains from Peru. Christopher Columbus, who learned that local tribes had been cultivating them for nearly 4 000 years, returned to Europe with one of the first shipments from the Americas in 1492. From Europe, chillies were taken to Africa, Asia and the Middle East, and everywhere they landed, they became a staple flavouring.

A few facts

- There are hundreds of varieties of chillies available today, with more than 200 identifiable varieties in Mexico alone.
- In 1912, there was a scale developed to measure the average hotness of chillies, created by Wilbur Scoville. The scale ran from 0 (sweet peppers) up to 300 000 for the hottest (habanero). Today, the Scoville units have been refined and run from 0–10.
- The attraction to hot, fiery food is down to the brain releasing endorphins, painkilling compounds which, at high levels, give a sensation of pleasure.
- The heat of a chilli comes from capsaicin, a compound found mainly in the ribs and seeds. This is why many recipes suggest that seeds are removed before adding the chilli.

Health & fitness

- Chillies contain more Vitamin C than many citrus fruits and also relieve nasal congestion.
- Scientists have recently found that eating chillies may cause the stomach to secrete a mucus that protects its lining against irritants such as acids.

Hints & tips

- When purchasing chillies, a rule of thumb is 'the fatter the chilli, the more mild it tends to be; the smaller, the hotter; and the darker the colour, the fiercer the bite'.
- Before handling chillies, lightly oil your fingers to form a barrier between your skin and the capsaicin. After chopping the chilli, simply wash your hands in warm, soapy water.

Pork curry
Burmese-style

Serves 4

675 g pork loin, cut into ±4 cm cubes

2.5 cm piece fresh root ginger, peeled and grated

6 fresh chillies, seeded and finely sliced (reduce this quantity by half for
   a milder version)

4 shallots or small onions, finely chopped

3 cloves garlic, crushed

30 ml brown sugar

10 ml turmeric

15 ml curry paste

15 ml sesame or corn oil

zest and juice of 1 lime

600 ml water or chicken stock

5 ml soy sauce

45 ml tamarind liquid or the juice and zest of 1 extra lime

15 ml Thai fish sauce (nam pla)

1. In a large bowl, mix the pork with the ginger, chillies, shallots,
   garlic, sugar, turmeric and curry paste.
2. In a heavy-based pan, heat the oil until hot, then add the
   pork mixture.
3. Stir thoroughly, then reduce the heat, cooking until the meat
   has changed colour and the curry is fragrant.
4. Add the remaining ingredients and bring to a simmer,
   stirring occasionally.
5. Cook for 18–20 minutes, or until the pork is tender.
6. Serve with Sweet-&-Sour Rice (page 100) or Sweet Potatoes Scented
   with Cumin (page 164).

Tomato

What's in a name?

There are several name traces for tomato: one is from the Aztec word *tomat*, meaning plump fruit, the other is *pommo d'oro*, or golden apple in Italian, referring to their original colour and firmness.

Historical notes

- Tomatoes may have originated in Peru and spread towards Mexico, where they became a staple of the Aztec diet.
- The Spanish brought the plant to Europe in the sixteenth century, where it was met with suspicion; many feared that they would transmit leprosy, and early cookbooks recommended that they be peeled and cooked for a minimum of 3 hours to render them edible. In the eighteenth century, the tomato began to be taken seriously and the red variety we know today was introduced. By 1835, the tomato was adopted by the USA, where millions of tonnes are grown and exported today.

A few facts

- The tomato is technically a fruit and not a vegetable, and is a relative of the nightshade family. Its other relatives include the pepper and the potato.
- There are over 1 000 different varieties, ranging in size and colour.
- The best flavoured tomatoes are those that have been left to mature on the vine.

Health & fitness

Tomatoes are a good source of carotenoids, potassium and vitamins C and E. They also contain very few calories. In fact, two medium-sized tomatoes contain around 22 calories (92 kJ) between them, and so are ideal to include in a weight-reducing diet.

Hints & tips

If you have an abundance of fresh seasonal tomatoes like I do, then one way to use them is to cook them down into a thick paste, cool, then strain and freeze the purée in an ice-cube tray. Once frozen, transfer to a freezer bag. When cooking, simply add a tomato cube whenever you need to boost the flavour of sauces, soups or gravies.

Tomato tarte tatin
with cheesy pastry
Serves 6

This tasty vegetarian dish makes an ideal lunch, hot or cold.

Tarte tatin
5 ml extra virgin olive oil

15 ml butter

5 ml castor sugar

8 small tomatoes, halved widthways

50 g fresh thyme

salt and freshly ground black pepper

400 g packet ready-made puff pastry
  or use the cheesy pastry recipe
  given here

150 g soft goat's cheese

50 g fresh basil leaves, shredded

Cheesy pastry
100 g plain (cake) flour

50 g butter

50 g Cheddar cheese, grated

4 spring onions

salt and freshly ground black pepper

1 egg yolk

1. Preheat the oven to 200 °C.
2. Heat the oil and butter in a 22–23 cm round ovenproof pan until the butter has melted.
3. Sprinkle the castor sugar into the pan and heat gently for 1–2 minutes until it starts to caramelize.
4. Place the tomatoes in the pan, cut side down, packing them tightly together. Sprinkle with the thyme, salt and pepper. Remove from the heat and keep aside.
5. If using ready-made pastry, move on to step 8. To make the cheesy pastry, place the flour, butter and cheese into a food processor and blitz until it forms a crumb-like texture.
6. Add the spring onions, salt and pepper and blitz briefly. Remove from the processor and place in a clean bowl.
7. Add the egg yolk and mix to form a ball, taking care not to overhandle the pastry. Wrap in clingfilm and refrigerate for 10 minutes before rolling out.
8. Divide the pastry into two and roll thinly to form discs measuring 23–24 cm wide, slightly larger than the pan.
9. Scatter pieces of goat's cheese and the basil leaves over one of the discs. Moisten the edge of the pastry with water, then place the second disc on top and seal.
10. Place the pastry on top of the tomatoes and press lightly to level off. Place in the oven and cook for 15–20 minutes, or until the pastry is golden.
11. When ready, remove from the oven and leave to cool for 5 minutes before turning out.
12. Serve with the Red-skinned Potato Salad with Lager Dressing (page 130).

25 minutes

Alan's bread & butter pudding
with pecans & whisky

Serves 4

50 g softened unsalted butter

8 slices one- or two-day-old white bread

3 large eggs, separated

75 g castor sugar

150 ml full-cream milk

185 ml double cream

1 ml grated nutmeg

1 ml ground allspice

25 g sultanas, soaked in 15 ml whisky

30 g pecan nuts, lightly crushed

5 ml icing sugar for dusting

cream or vanilla ice cream for serving

1. Preheat the oven to 180 °C.
2. Butter the base and sides of four single-serving ramekins and butter the bread.
3. Cut the bread into circles the same size as the ramekins.
4. Place the egg yolks and half the castor sugar into a bowl and whisk until pale and light.
5. Heat the milk and cream in a pan until warm. Remove from the heat and pour the mixture over the eggs and sugar. Whisk continuously while adding the spices.
6. In a separate grease-free bowl, whisk the egg whites until soft peak stage, then sprinkle in the remaining castor sugar, whisking continuously.
7. Fold the egg whites into the custard mixture until well incorporated and light.
8. Place a layer of bread onto the base of the ramekins, followed by a scattering of soaked sultanas, then pour over the egg-custard mix until the bread is submerged.
9. Repeat this process until all the bread, sultanas and custard have been used.
10. Sprinkle over the pecans and dust lightly with the icing sugar.
11. Place in the oven and cook for 22–25 minutes.
12. When ready, remove from the oven and dust with a little more icing sugar. Serve immediately with cream or ice cream.

25 minutes

Apple

What's in a name?

The first cultivated apples seem to have been called 'abel', and variations of this word developed as the fruit spread across Europe. The Anglo-Saxons called it 'aeppel', which gradually developed into the modern word.

Historical notes

Apples were one of the earliest cultivated fruits, with a domesticated history dating back 4 000 years. The original apples were very small in size, very sour and similar to our modern-day crab apples. The Romans improved cultivation and contributed to the distribution of this much-loved fruit. In later years, well-known varieties were grown throughout the world, such as Cox's orange pippin invented by Mr Cox in 1830, a keen gardener who lived at what is now Heathrow Airport; and Granny Smiths, created by Maria Ann Smith, an English midwife's daughter who settled in Australia in 1838.

A few facts

- There are said to be well over 10 000 different varieties of apple identified internationally.
- America loves the apple and even named New York 'the Big Apple'.
- The United Kingdom once put more than 1 million apples on display at Bingley Hall to celebrate the great seasonal crop.
- In French cookery, anything described as 'à la Normand' includes apples.

Health & fitness

- Apples are a good source of Vitamin C, which helps to maintain the immune system.
- In alternative medicine, ripe uncooked apples were traditionally used for treating constipation, while their stewed form was eaten to treat diarrhoea and gastro-enteritis.

Hints & tips

If baking apples or cooking them in a microwave, always make a small incision around the apple, three-quarters up towards the core end. This will prevent the apple from bursting as the incision will act as a release valve for the escaping steam.

Baked apples
with honey & hazelnuts

Serves 4 (this recipe is easily doubled)

4 small cooking apples, cored

25 ml butter

50 g sultanas, roughly chopped

50 g mixed dried candied fruit peel (orange, lemon, lime and grapefruit),
   roughly chopped

50 g hazelnuts, roasted and roughly chopped

80 g dark brown (muscavado) sugar

30 ml clear honey

2.5 ml grated nutmeg

150 ml cider

30 ml brandy

Lime or Ginger Cream (page 150) for serving

1. Preheat the oven to 180 °C.
2. Using the point of a small knife, insert it into the skin of the apples, about three-quarters to the top, and slit all around, piercing the skin only. Keep aside.
3. In a bowl, mix together the butter, sultanas, dried fruit peel, nuts and sugar and stuff each apple with the mixture, until full and tight.
4. Place the apples in an ovenproof dish and drizzle over the honey. Dust with the nutmeg.
5. Pour the cider and brandy around the apples and then cover the dish with foil.
6. Bake for 20 minutes.
7. Remove the foil, increase the oven temperature to 200 °C and cook for a further 5 minutes.
8. Serve the apples with the pan juices drizzled over and a little Lime or Ginger Cream.

This section is ideal if you have a little more time to play in the kitchen. The dishes are great for entertaining or dinner parties.

thirty

30
minutes
cooking time

Rooibos tea-poached trout
with apples & sultanas

A great dish for lunch or dinner.

1 x 300 g whole trout per person (head on or off)
2 bay leaves
6 black peppercorns
juice and zest of 1 lemon
50 ml cider vinegar or white wine vinegar
250 ml fresh brewed Rooibos tea
2 dessert apples, peeled, cored and sliced
60 g sultanas
30 ml demerara sugar
salt and freshly ground black pepper

1. Preheat the oven to 180 °C.
2. Place the fish into a shallow ovenproof dish and add the bay leaves and peppercorns.
3. Pour over the lemon juice, zest, cider vinegar and tea.
4. Scatter over the sliced apples and sultanas.
5. Sprinkle over the brown sugar, salt and pepper and cover with a lid or foil.
6. Place in the oven and cook for 25–28 minutes.
7. Serve the fish with a crisp salad and dressing of choice (pages 33–34).

30 minutes

Chicken breasts
stuffed with basil, ham & cheese
Serves 4

A good family meal that also works well with chicken thighs.

30 ml grated Parmesan cheese

75 g ricotta cheese

1 small egg yolk

about 12 fresh basil leaves, torn in half

10 ml basil pesto

2.5 ml each salt and freshly ground black pepper

4 x 180 g chicken breast fillets (or 4 large deboned thighs)

4 large slices Parma or smoked ham

25 g butter

150 ml dry white wine

1. Preheat the oven to 200 °C.
2. In a bowl, mix together the Parmesan, ricotta, egg yolk, basil leaves, basil pesto and salt and pepper.
3. Make incisions in the sides of the chicken breasts and open flat, and batten out lightly.
4. Spread the stuffing evenly over the chicken and fold over to re-form the chicken breast.
5. Wrap the ham around the outside of the chicken to make neat parcels (secure with a toothpick if necessary).
6. Melt the butter in a shallow, ovenproof casserole. When foaming, add the chicken and fry lightly on both sides.
7. Add the wine and cover the dish.
8. Place in the oven and cook for 25 minutes, or until tender.

Olive oil

What's in a name?

The word 'oil' comes directly from the Latin *oleum*, meaning olive oil, as this would have been the first variety of oil ever produced.

Historical notes

- Olive oil was being pressed around the Mediterranean 5 000 years ago and was once used to anoint kings, bishops and popes to confirm their authority and status.
- The Greeks felled their native forests and built an entire export industry around olive oil in 600 BC.
- The Romans became such connoisseurs of the fruit that they were able to identify the provenance of olives and the oil blindfolded, a skill that became a party game at social banquets.
- The olive branch is traditionally a symbol of both peace and fertility.

A few facts

Approximately 90 per cent of the world's olive production is used to make olive oil; the remaining 10 per cent is processed to become table olives.

Health & fitness

- Olive oil has a healthy image due to the fact that it is high in monounsaturated fatty acids. These do not adversely affect blood cholesterol and, according to some scientific studies, may even help to lower blood cholesterol levels.
- Olive oil is also a good source of Vitamin E, which plays a vital protective role. However, this benefit can be lost if the oil is stored in direct sunlight.

Hints & tips

- It is pointless using a good quality virgin oil for cooking, as it will destroy the delicate flavour of the oil and waste your money at the same time. A cheaper quality will suffice for cooking with no adverse effect whatsoever.
- Save the finer quality and more expensive varieties for dressing and drizzling.

Marmalade-basted chicken
with enraged oil
Serves 4

A tasty family meal, but the oil option is for adults only!

4 chicken leg joints (leg and thigh),
　skin removed for healthier option
salt and freshly ground black pepper
15 ml olive oil
60 ml extra thick-cut marmalade
50 g fresh mint leaves, chopped
zest of 1 large orange
3 cloves garlic, finely chopped

Enraged oil
250 ml olive oil plus 15 ml for frying
4 fresh hot red chillies, roughly
　chopped with seeds
pinch of salt
15 ml tomato paste

The beauty of this hot, spicy oil is that, while it may take 30 minutes to cook, it will last up to four weeks. The oil has a reddish colour and wonderful roasted chilli aroma.

1. If using, make the enraged oil first.
2. Heat the 15 ml olive oil in an ovenproof pan.
3. Add the chopped chillies to the hot pan and fry over gentle heat for 2–3 minutes.
4. Add a pinch of salt and the tomato paste and stir well.
5. Gradually stir in the remaining olive oil, a little at a time, then bring to the boil.
6. Reduce the heat and simmer gently for 20 minutes.
7. Switch off the heat and leave to cool.
8. Pass the cooled oil through a muslin cloth or clean tea towel and pour into a sterilized bottle. Keep aside until ready to use.
9. Preheat the oven to 200 °C.
10. Sprinkle the chicken joints with salt and pepper.
11. Drizzle the oil onto a roasting tray, then place the chicken pieces on the tray.
12. In a bowl, mix together the marmalade, mint, orange zest, garlic and a little more seasoning and mix thoroughly.
13. Spread this mixture all over the chicken joints.
14. Place into the oven and cook for 25–30 minutes, or until cooked through.
15. When ready, serve drizzled with a little enraged oil, a fresh orange salad and a little Sweet-&-Sour Rice (page 100).

30 minutes

158

Lamb pie
with pear & rosemary
Serves 4–6

60 g unsalted butter

2 leeks (15 cm) or 1½ medium onions, sliced

2.5 ml chopped fresh thyme

2.5 ml chopped fresh rosemary

salt and freshly ground black pepper

450 g lamb mince

30 g brown sugar or finely chopped candied or dried pear

25 g plain (cake) flour

90 g currants

200 ml red wine

5 ml tomato paste

1 pear, peeled, cored and chopped

350 g ready-made puff pastry

1 egg, lightly beaten

1. Preheat the oven to 180 °C.
2. Melt the butter in a heavy-based pan.
3. Add the sliced leeks or onions, cover the pan and cook gently for 2–3 minutes.
4. Add the herbs, salt and pepper, mince and the sugar or candied pear and stir well.
5. Cover again and cook for 3–4 minutes.
6. Add the flour and stir well, cooking for a couple more minutes.
7. Add the currants, followed by the wine, tomato paste and chopped pear, and switch off the heat. Leave to cool.
8. Meanwhile, divide the pastry in two. Roll out one half of the pastry to 3–4 mm thick and use this to line a lightly greased 25 cm flan ring.
9. Roll out the other half (the pastry lid) to 3–4 mm thick and keep aside.
10. Brush the rim of the pastry sides with a little of the beaten egg.
11. Fill the lined flan ring with the mince mixture, level it off and cover with the pastry lid, sticking the sides and lid together.
12. Crimp the edge, brush the top with more egg wash and place in the oven for 22–25 minutes.
13. When cooked, remove from the oven to cool slightly, then cut and serve.

Lamb cutlets
with wow wow sauce
Serves 4

2 x 6-bone racks of lamb, trimmed
(allow 3–4 cutlets per portion)
20 ml prepared English Mustard
5 ml cayenne pepper
salt and freshly ground black pepper
60 g butter, melted
180 g fine fresh breadcrumbs

Wow wow sauce
50 g butter
25 g plain (cake) flour
275–300 ml chicken stock
30 ml white wine vinegar
5 ml prepared English mustard
15 ml port wine
15 ml finely chopped fresh flat-leaf
parsley
6 gherkins or pickled walnuts,
chopped
30 ml sultanas

1. Preheat the oven to 200 °C.
2. Brush or spread the mustard all over the lamb, then dust all over with cayenne pepper, salt and black pepper.
3. Brush with melted butter, then roll in the breadcrumbs.
4. Stand the racks in a lightly greased roasting pan and place in the oven.
5. Cook for 10–12 minutes, then turn the heat down to 160 °C and cook for a further 10 minutes. This should see the racks cooked to medium-rare.
6. While the lamb is in the oven, make the sauce. Melt the butter in a heavy-based pan over a gentle heat.
7. Add the flour and cook gently for 2–3 minutes, stirring continuously.
8. In a separate pan, warm the stock and, little by little, add the flour and butter mixture, stirring continuously until you have a smooth consistency that lightly coats the back of the spoon.
9. Add the vinegar, mustard and port and bring to a simmer. (If there are any lumps, simply strain the liquid into a clean pan.)
10. Add the chopped parsley, gherkins or walnuts, and sultanas.
11. Remove the lamb from the oven and leave to rest for 10 minutes before carving and serving with the wow wow sauce. Pan Haggerty Potatoes (page 120) or Sweet Potatoes Scented with Cumin (page 164) work well with this dish.

30 minutes

162

Poached fillet of beef
with pumpkin-mustard cream sauce

Serves 4

1 litre chicken stock

150 g pumpkin or butternut, peeled,
 seeded and cut into small pieces

50 g carrots, chopped

4 x 175 g beef fillet steaks (about
 5 cm thick)

15 ml prepared English mustard

100 ml double cream

salt and freshly ground black pepper

1. Place the stock in a large pan with the pumpkin
 or butternut and the carrots and bring to a simmer.
2. Add the steaks and poach gently for 8–10 minutes.
3. Remove the beef from the pan, cover and keep warm.
4. Bring the stock back to the boil and add the mustard
 and cream. Stir and simmer for 2 minutes.
5. Pour the liquid and vegetables into a food processor
 and blitz until it forms a smooth sauce. Season.
6. Place the steaks in the centre of each warmed bowl
 and drizzle with the sauce. Serve with vegetables.

Italian Parmesan risotto

Serves 4

1 medium onion, finely chopped

90 g butter

2 cloves garlic, crushed

350 g Arborio rice

150 ml dry white wine

1 litre boiling vegetable stock

90 g Parmesan cheese, grated

salt and freshly ground black pepper

45 ml chopped fresh flat-leaf parsley

1. Sweat off the onion in half the butter and cook gently for 2–3 minutes until translucent – do not let it colour.
2. Add the garlic, then the rice and stir well for a further 1–2 minutes.
3. Add the wine and bring to a simmer.
4. Add the boiling stock a little at a time, stirring regularly for around 20–25 minutes.
5. When all the stock has been absorbed, add the Parmesan cheese and the remaining butter.
6. Stir thoroughly and season.
7. Divide the risotto among four bowls, sprinkle the parsley over the top, and serve.

Sweet potatoes
scented with cumin

Serves 4–6

1.6 kg sweet potatoes, washed, peeled and cut into pieces

15 ml dry-roasted ground cumin

200 ml corn oil

100 g butter

1. Preheat the oven to 200 °C.
2. Parboil the sweet potatoes in lightly salted water for 3–5 minutes. Dry thoroughly.
3. Dust the potatoes with the cumin.
4. In an ovenproof pan, heat the oil and butter together until very hot.
5. Add the potatoes and roll and turn them in the hot oil for 3–4 minutes.
6. Place in the oven for around 20–25 minutes.
7. Serve with a little butter or a dollop of crème fraîche or plain yoghurt.

Noodle tart
scented with bacon & cardamom
Serves 4

200 g sweet pastry (see recipe given
   here) or use ready-made pastry

butter for greasing tartlet tins

6 egg yolks

140 g castor sugar

275 ml double cream

5 ml ground cardamom seeds

150 ml water

4 rashers rindless bacon, cut in
   thin strips

150 g cooked noodles (rice noodles,
   leftover vermicelli or linguine
   work well)

Sweet pastry (makes 275 g)

150 g plain (cake) flour

pinch of salt

75 g chilled unsalted butter, cut into
   1 cm cubes

25 g icing sugar

2 egg yolks

zest of 1 lemon

1. If using ready-made pastry, move on to step 6.
   To make the pastry yourself, sift the flour and salt
   to make a mound on a chilled work surface.

2. Make a well in the centre and add the butter and
   sugar. Add the egg yolks and the zest.

3. Using your fingertips, mix together the butter, yolks
   and sugar until it resembles scrambled egg.

4. Bring in the flour bit by bit and work it quickly until
   it has all been incorporated. Knead the dough lightly
   for 1 minute until smooth, then shape it into a flat
   round, wrap in clingfilm and refrigerate for 1 hour.

5. Preheat the oven to 180 °C.

6. Divide the pastry into four and roll out to 3 mm thick.
   Line 4 x 15 cm buttered tartlet tins with the pastry.

7. Place greaseproof paper or foil in each and weigh down
   with dried beans. Place on a baking tray and bake blind
   for 3–4 minutes. Discard the paper and beans.

8. To make the filling, beat the egg yolks with 50 g
   castor sugar until light and creamy.

9. Warm the cream and cardamom in a pan over a gentle
   heat. Bring to a simmer, then switch off the heat. Pour
   the cream mixture gradually over the egg mixture,
   stirring continuously until well incorporated.

10. Place the remaining castor sugar and the water into
    a wok or large pan and bring to a simmer. Cook for
    2–3 minutes until slightly syrupy.

11. Place the bacon in the boiling syrup for 2 minutes.
    Add this to the cooked pasta and stir well to coat.

12. Divide the precooked noodles among the tartlet cases.
    Pour over the egg mixture to the brim, and bake for
    12–15 minutes. Serve warm, with vanilla ice cream.

30 minutes

166

Ginger

What's in a name?

The word ginger comes from the Sanskrit *smga – veram*, meaning horn root, which eventually developed into the Latin *zingiber*, then into the Old English *gingifer*.

Historical notes

- Ginger was originally grown in Bengal and Malabar in India and has also been used in China for thousands of years.
- The ancient Egyptians used it in a spiced honey cake, and a baker on the Greek island of Rhodes apparently created the first ever gingerbread. This soon spread to the Roman Empire where the Roman legions enjoyed it so much that they would carry it on their long journeys and conquests to sustain them along the way.
- During the Dark Ages, when few people had access to spices, gingerbread was made in monasteries. Breadcrumbs formulated the basis of the medieval recipe and the mixture was then pressed into a square mould that resulted in a solid, spicy slab.

A few facts

- Fresh root ginger, closely related to turmeric, is an underground stem from which stubby fingers are formed, topped with small buds. The roots are cut off before marketing.
- Fresh root ginger will keep for weeks and even months in the right conditions, providing that it is kept in a cool, dark environment with the skin intact.

Health & fitness

- Ginger helps digestion and is a popular remedy for nausea. It is often used to help treat morning sickness and motion sickness and is taken as a tea infusion.
- Historically, it was chewed to help relieve toothache as well as stimulate the liver to remove toxins.

Hints & tips

When peeling fresh root ginger, simply use a teaspoon to scrape away the very thin skin. This saves a great deal of time and prevents waste.

Poached peaches
in ginger syrup
Serves 4

500 ml water

300 g sugar

grated zest and juice of 1 medium orange

2 sticks cinnamon

5 cm piece fresh root ginger

3 whole cloves

125 ml dry white wine

45 ml brandy or schnapps

1 bay leaf

8 just ripe peaches (do not peel)

1. Place all the ingredients, with the exception of the peaches, into a saucepan and bring to the boil, stirring until the sugar dissolves.
2. Simmer the liquid for 5 minutes.
3. Remove from the heat and allow to cool slightly, then lower the peaches into the poaching liquid. Ensure that the peaches are fully submerged (this will depend on the size of the saucepan – the smaller the better, but it will need to be able to hold all eight peaches).
4. Return to the heat and bring to a simmer, then reduce the heat and poach gently for 8–10 minutes. (The duration will depend upon the ripeness of the peaches.)
5. When the peaches are soft, switch off the heat and leave them to cool in the syrup.
6. Once cooled, remove the skin with a small knife and return the peaches to the syrup.
7. Serve them either warm or cold, with a little Lime or Ginger Cream (page 150).

Normandy apple tart

Serves 4

150 g ready-made puff pastry

50 g butter

50 g castor sugar

1 egg yolk

50 g ground almonds

4 red apples, cored and very finely sliced (you need 12–15 slices from each apple)

50 g icing sugar

1. Preheat the oven to 200 °C.
2. Roll the pastry into a circular shape 4–5 mm thick and prick with a fork. Place on a lightly greased oven tray.
3. Cream the butter and castor sugar together until light and fluffy, then add the egg yolk and mix well.
4. Add the ground almonds and mix thoroughly.
5. Spread a thin, even layer of the almond cream over the pastry. Place the slices of apple in a circular pattern on the pastry circle, slightly overlapping the slices.
6. Sprinkle with the icing sugar, then place into the oven for around 25 minutes, or until golden and crisp.
7. Serve hot or warm with a little cream or ice cream.

30 minutes

Rosemary

What's in a name?

Rosemary gets its name from the Latin *ros marinus*, meaning dew of the sea, possibly due to the fact that it grows particularly well near water.

Historical notes

- Rosemary was a firm favourite of ancient herdsmen, as their goats would only devour the fresh young shoots and not the whole shrub, ensuring a constant and permanent supply of food.
- It was also traditionally seen as a symbol of friendship and remembrance and was used at both weddings and funerals.
- Medieval students used to wear wreaths in their hair when taking exams, as it was thought to stimulate the memory.

A few facts

- Rosemary is an evergreen perennial shrub, native to the Mediterranean. It can grow up to 1.5 m in height and grows as well in a pot as it does in the ground.
- Rosemary's uses are far and wide, ranging from flavouring stews and casseroles, lamb and rabbit, to scallops and prawns to salads and chocolate.
- The branches add a lovely fragrance to barbecue coals.

Health & fitness

- Rosemary is said to act as a stimulant to both the nervous and circulatory systems.
- It helps to soothe the digestive system by relieving indigestion, and a tea infusion also makes a good antiseptic gargle for sore throats.

Hints & tips

Use thick rosemary branches as skewers for the barbecue. They impart a wonderful flavour to the skewered meat or vegetables.

Baked rosemary custard
Serves 4

150 ml sweet white wine

150 ml full-cream milk

350 ml double cream

15 ml chopped fresh rosemary

100 g butter

6 medium egg yolks

50 g castor sugar

1. Preheat the oven to 140 °C.
2. Place the wine, milk, cream, rosemary and butter into a pan and heat gently, stirring until the butter has melted.
3. Remove from the heat and keep aside for 10 minutes.
4. Whisk together the egg yolks and castor sugar until light and creamy. Strain the milk and cream mixture into the egg and sugar mix, stirring constantly.
5. Return the mixture to the pan and cook, stirring gently over a low heat, until the mixture coats the back of the spoon. Do not let it boil as it will curdle.
6. Pour the custards into 4 x 150 ml ovenproof ramekins and place in the oven for 25 minutes.
7. Serve either just warm or chilled.

Exotic fruit brûlée
Serves 4

4 large egg yolks

55 g castor sugar

2.5 ml grated nutmeg

500 ml double cream

½ small ripe mango, peeled, stoned, and thinly sliced

1 small fig, sliced (do not peel)

1 fresh peach, stoned, and sliced (do not peel)

½ banana, sliced

20 ml brandy

60 ml brown sugar for glazing

4 Cape gooseberries to decorate

1. Preheat the oven to 180 °C.
2. Beat the egg yolks, castor sugar and nutmeg until light.
3. Heat the cream in a pan until simmering gently.
4. Divide the prepared fruit among 4 x 200 ml ramekins and sprinkle with the brandy.
5. Stir the warm cream into the egg mixture, then pour this over the fruit.
6. Place the ramekins in a roasting pan, then pour hot water to halfway up the sides of the ramekins. Place in the oven for 25–30 minutes, or until set.
7. Sprinkle with the brown sugar and place under a preheated grill (or use a blowtorch) until the sugar caramelizes. Top with a gooseberry and serve.

Conversion charts

Celsius (°C)	Fahrenheit (°F)	Gas mark
100 °C	200 °F	¼
110 °C	225 °F	¼
120 °C	250 °F	½
140 °C	275 °F	1
150 °C	300 °F	2
160 °C	325 °F	3
180 °C	350 °F	4
190 °C	375 °F	5
200 °C	400 °F	6
220 °C	425 °F	7
230 °C	450 °F	8
240 °C	475 °F	9

Metric	US cups	Imperial
5 ml	1 tsp	³⁄₁₆ fl oz
15 ml	1 Tbsp	½ fl oz
60 ml	4 Tbsp (¼ cup)	2 fl oz
80 ml	⅓ cup	2¾ fl oz
125 ml	½ cup	4½ fl oz
160 ml	⅔ cup	5½ fl oz
200 ml	¾ cup	7 fl oz
250 ml	1 cup	9 fl oz
100 g	–	3½ oz
250 g	–	9 oz
500 g	–	1 lb
750 g	–	1¾ lb
1 kg	–	2¼ lb

Mass comparison: equal to 250 ml (1 cup)

Breadcrumbs (fresh)	60 g		Fruit (dried)	150 g
Breadcrumbs (dried)	120 g		Flour (cake, white bread	
Butter or margarine	230 g		or brown bread)	140 g
Cheese (grated Cheddar)	100 g		Honey or syrup	250 g
Cheese (grated mozzarella)	125 g		Nuts (whole)	100 g
Cheese (cream or cottage)	250 g		Nuts (chopped)	150 g
Cocoa powder	100 g		Sugar (granulated)	200 g
Coconut (desiccated)	80 g		Sugar (castor)	210 g
Fruit (dates or cake mix)	150 g		Sugar (icing)	130 g